MORE
THORNY
PROBLEMS

Also by Helen Yemm

Gardening from Scratch: Vol 2 (with Jojo Norris and Gay Search)

Gardening in Your Nightie: What Every Passionate Gardener
Should Know, But Never Dared to Ask

RHS Grow Your Own Flowers

Thorny Problems: A Seasonal Collection of Gardening Queries and
Answers from *The Daily Telegraph*'s Much-loved Columnist

Gardening in Pyjamas: Horticultural Enlightenment
for Obsessive Dawn Raiders

The Daily Telegraph

MORE
THORNY
PROBLEMS

All-new compilation of seasonal questions
and answers from *The Daily Telegraph*'s
much-loved gardening columnist

HELEN YEMM

SIMON &
SCHUSTER
ILLUSTRATED

London · New York · Sydney · Toronto · New Delhi

A CBS COMPANY

First published in Great Britain by Simon & Schuster UK Ltd, 2014
A CBS COMPANY

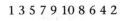

1 3 5 7 9 10 8 6 4 2

SIMON & SCHUSTER
ILLUSTRATED BOOKS
Simon & Schuster UK Ltd
222 Gray's Inn Road
London WC1X 8HB

www.simonandschuster.co.uk

Simon & Schuster Australia, Sydney
Simon & Schuster India, New Delhi

A CIP catalogue record for this book is
available from the British Library

ISBN 978-1-47113-670-2

Illustrations by Francine Lawrence
Designed and typeset by Richard Proctor
Edited by Sharon Amos
Printed and bound in the UK by
CPI Group (UK) Ltd, Croydon CR0 4YY

Contents

DEDICATION

For my son (and long-suffering IT advisor) Henry,
despite the fact that he decided to go off around the
world while I put this together.

Introduction

Presumably you already know the score. I can't imagine anyone who has got as far as reading the introduction to a book entitled *More Thorny Problems* has not read the first volume, or is not at least familiar with the Thorny Problems page – the letters page (actually a half-page, the other half being smothered in advertisements) – in *The Daily Telegraph*'s Saturday Gardening supplement.

The success of the original Thorny Problems book took me by surprise, selling to both regular *Telegraph* Gardening devotees (who presumably got what they expected), as well as to the wider gardening public, who very possibly did not. It was just a distillation, of course, of the 'worst' of the first years of Thorny Problems, reorganised to make it into a seasonally helpful practical book. Three years have passed since it was published and the emails and 'proper' letters have kept on coming in (although the latter have of course thinned out a bit as almost a whole generation has moved with the times and gone online, while the oldies who wouldn't or couldn't do so have started to drop off their perches). And I, too, somewhat against the odds perhaps in these unpredictable times, have kept on dishing out the Thorny Problems advice. So here we are again, with another batch of gardening questions and my attempts at enlightenment and reassurance, based, as often as possible, on my own experiences, both positive and negative. A few common problems that inevitably come up year after year are of course re-visited, but I have tried to approach them from a different angle and with some new ideas, based on my still-growing experience.

Most of the time, it is the sheer good humour and enthusiasm of readers that keeps me going and makes my job worthwhile but there are times, I confess, when my enthusiasm for ladling out constant helpings of encouragement and common-sense advice has been known to wear a bit thin. Well, wouldn't yours have done so, dear readers, during and after dark and freezing winters, when I had to subsist on an almost daily diet of miserable e-wails accompanied by wretched digital pictures of dead bay trees and other grotesque horticultural moribundia? I have actually gained a reputation for sometimes getting quite ratty. In print, even. You'll see.

The widespread use of the internet now has made a subtle difference to the way I have to deal with the weekly page: as often as not, by the time gardeners get as far as writing to me, they have already scrolled down through yards of 'best practice' gardening advice from pundits, visited online amateur gardening forums that offer sometimes terrifyingly contradictory (and, frankly, occasionally quite batty) advice and, throwing their hands up in horror at the sheer amount of information available to them, they turn to me to ask me what I think they should do. All of which makes me feel that I am putting my head on a block every Saturday morning.

So here you have it. Head on block. A whole book of it.

Helen Yemm
March 2014

❧ Spring ❧

March

Welcome to March, the start of a whole new *Thorny Problems*-style gardening year. Here and in subsequent chapters you will find responses to letters from *Telegraph* readers about real-life-and-death gardening quandaries and commonly experienced mishaps – how to rescue wilting things, when (or not) to lop and chop and how to tackle nasty-looking bugs and thugs. You may find yourself enlightened by seasonally appropriate hints and tips, by basic explanation of key issues, with complicated horticulture kept to the minimum, as little jargon or Latin as I can get away with and using English plant names wherever possible.

You may be simply reassured by the fact that you have the same problems out there as everyone else, comforted (and just a little smug, maybe) that on the whole you get things right. Most savvy gardeners, after all, have learned the hard way how to face each growing season bravely, armed with a powerful combination of ever-growing experience, a dollop of pragmatism, lots of good intentions, a measure of tolerance and maybe (though less frequently than heretofore) a spray bottle of something really vile-smelling and potent. And they always acknowledge the need to keep their fingers firmly crossed, taking the capriciousness of Mother Nature into account. Things are bound to be better or at least different this year, after all...

Alternatively you could be one of those for whom gardening is considered, grudgingly, to be obligatory extra-mural drudgery, something to be fitted in between work, golf, the gym and shopping – and in the summertime only. For such innocents, the garden is principally a place into which to pitch the children and their footballs

and monstrous plastic play paraphernalia, hoping against hope that whatever they get up to out there won't systematically destroy neighbourly relations or worse, adversely affect the value of the property. There is usually a preparatory spring clear-up of some sort around now, aimed at creating a space where the occasional evening tincture can be enjoyed between weather fronts during the summer, and in a month or so you may want to add some 'colour'.

If you belong to the latter, you may have picked up this slim volume looking for a magic formula: gardening by numbers, starting in Month Number Three. Well keep going. You may even find that reading suggested solutions to other people's dire and dodgy outdoor mis-happenings, rather than staring uncomprehendingly at perfection-gardening on telly or flicking, dazed, through old glossy mags left on the train, might just possibly do the trick.

SNOWDROPS OR SLOWDROPS?

How can I encourage my small colony of snowdrops,
planted by me four years ago, to increase more quickly?
I am tempted to deadhead each flower so that all of each
plant's energy goes into making more and better bulbs.
Janet, by email

It is best, I think, to let the snowdrops get on with it without too much upheaval.

Almost all snowdrops multiply naturally through a combination of producing offsets (small bulbs attached to the 'parent' bulb) each year and by ripening seed. An exception to this is the most common double-flowered snowdrop (*Galanthus nivalis* f. *pleniflorus* 'Flore Pleno'). This one does not set seed, so only spreads via its offsets. Offsets themselves do not produce flowers for a couple of years or more.

Rather than deadheading, just let heavy snowdrop seed heads droop on to the ground and they will release their seed heads once they ripen during the summer. Self-sown seedlings just show as a tiny pair of leaves in their first year and take even longer than offsets to get going, but your colony will, without any intervention on your part, gradually bulk up.

It would be helpful if you mark out a cultivation no-go area around the clumps so that this process has a chance to happen without disturbance. It is easy to forget where spring-flowering bulbs are, once their leaves have vanished. 🌿

RADICAL CLEMATIS PRUNING

Hesitant pruner Annette's clematis are all over the place. Literally. Can she really prune the late-flowering ones down to 'knee-height' as instructed? Yes she can. And if you give a previously somewhat abandoned mature clematis this treatment, it will react by producing numerous shoots from below ground level. Hard-pruning like this is also the best way to renovate neglected early-flowerers ('The President' and co), but of course they will not flower properly for a year afterwards. However, for the late-flowerers there is something I call 'strategic pruning' – which means that you can prune them to make them achieve what you want them to. If you grow one to glorify a large tree ('Bill MacKenzie' looks good grown aloft – yellow flowers followed by silky seeds), you could prune it back to the top of the tree's trunk – so that the new shoots can easily get into the canopy – rather than cut to 'knee-height' and make it start the upward clamber from ground level each year. March is a bit late for clematis pruning, but for Annette, it is probably a case of 'better late than never'.

PLEA FROM A WEARY WEEDER

*Thistles and grass have invaded my son's long, narrow
boundary border where he planted trees and shrubs a year
ago. The invasion is unavoidable, as there is an unkempt
meadow on the other side of the fence. I hand-weed the bed
carefully for him from time to time, but have had enough.
What can I use to get rid of the invaders, or at least slow
them down?*
Lisa, by email

Much of the problem will be caused by thistledown and other
seeds being blown into the garden from the field. I had a
similar problem in my old garden, and it can never be
completely eliminated – although a charm offensive on the
owner of the field, hoping that he/she will 'top' it in summer
before the thistles flower may help a bit.

If this is an open post-and-rail fence, a barrier of some
kind attached to the bottom of it might be helpful – the sort
of thing sold as temporary wind protection for new hedges
(less obtrusive in black if you can get it). Instead of hand
weeding, you could also knobble individual young thistle
seedlings and grass clumps with glyphosate (as in Roundup),
armed with a small sprayer and using a cut-off drinks bottle
as a protective cowl. And a very thick mulch of bark over the
whole area in early spring will help prevent seed germination.

Maybe you can take comfort from the fact that as the
shrubs establish deep roots, thicken up and cover more
ground, the space that these weeds have grabbed between
them will become slightly less inviting – drier and with little
light. You and your son may only have to fight for the upper
hand in the relatively short term. 🌿

TIME TO DIVIDE HOSTAS

Caroline wants to know how and when she should split some large hostas that have grown too big for their containers. Any time when they are dormant is fine, but I find it easiest to do it when their fat, pointed new shoots are quite clearly visible close to the soil surface. When she de-pots her hostas she will discover a dense, matted root system that it is impossible not to damage. However, sawn cleanly into pieces (an old bread knife is useful), the plant will not come to any harm and as long as each division has several strong undamaged shoots, the plant should grow well during the coming growing season in fresh compost (John Innes No 3, plus some compost) and more space in which to expand.

PLANTS IN AN OLD WATER TANK

I have a galvanised water tank 29 × 22in and 22in deep (74 × 57 × 57cm), in which I would like to grow some long-term plants. The tank will be sited in a south-facing position, in a sometimes-blowy coastal garden in Anglesey. Have you any planting suggestions? I favour lavender. And which John Innes planting medium should I use?
Denise, by email

This sounds fun – but I think there are several things to think about here:
1. You do not need the entire depth for plant roots. Put about 6in (15cm) of broken polystyrene packaging in the base of the tank first, then a sheet of plastic (perforated a few times) or weed-smothering membrane on top, between the polystyrene and the compost.
2. Insulate the planting area of the tank with bubble wrap (inside the tank). Metal containers can get extremely hot (or cold) and this will go some way towards preventing roots from baking or freezing.
3. Use John Innes No 3, which is the nearest to good garden

soil. Add a little (about 15 per cent) multi-purpose compost or leaf mould if you have it, to open up the texture a bit; but if you are planting lavender (or other Mediterranean plants) don't enrich the soil too much.

4. Choose your lavender carefully. Two or three plants of a compact variety ('Hidcote') would look better than one whopper.

5. Other plants that would enjoy the same soil/conditions and look good in the galvanised metal container are purple sage (*Salvia officinalis* 'Purpurascens') or prostrate rosemary (*Rosmarinus officinalis* Prostratus Group). An even tougher, wind-tolerant ever-grey that would also look good is *Brachyglottis monroi*. 🌿

SOMEONE'S FOR THE CHOP

Last spring, my garden helper misunderstood my instructions and cut a young black-leaved elder to the ground. I grow this shrub (in a rather tight space) partly for its pretty pink flowers. Eventually the shrub made several straight, very healthy shoots almost a metre tall, but no flowers. What should I do now?
'Slightly Peeved', by email

A smart move might be not to let anyone else loose on it. Even some gardeners who spell the word with a capital G, when faced with the leafless growth of a deciduous shrub, feel utterly compelled to 'tidy it up'. This is all very fine if the shrub in question is something like a hypericum or a buddleja, that flowers late in the season on new growth, or if it is grown simply for the beauty of its foliage. But with those that are grown for their spring flowers, it can be little short of disaster – if only in the short term.

    Sambucus nigra 'Eva' (formerly known as 'Black Lace') would naturally grow to around 10ft by 6ft (3 × 1.8m) if left to its own devices. You are therefore going to have to control its growth quite cleverly in a tight space, pruning it hard each year immediately after it has flowered. It will then make new shoots that if left well alone will flower for you the following

spring. The brutal chop it received last spring did you a favour in one sense, by creating a rather good low framework that will make management of it easy in the future. This spring I would leave at least half of the shoots intact so that they will flower, and cut the remainder down by two-thirds. Follow this kind of routine in the future in order to keep its growth within bounds while still benefitting from its flowers.

(Perhaps I should add here that the pink flowers of this beautiful black-leaved elder make pink elderflower cordial.) 🌿

RE-WEEDING BETWEEN THE LINES

Janet 'read somewhere' about a special sand that can be used when laying or renovating paving that will inhibit the growth of weeds. Having myself drawn a blank on the matter and advised Janet to try all sorts of other methods to get control of the weeds between her paving stones, horticultural *eminence grise* Peter Seabrook and fellow readers John and Chris came to the rescue. They told me the product is called Dansand and contains a growth-inhibiting combination of dried silica sand and special minerals that have a naturally high pH value and create desert-like conditions to help prevent weed growth and germination. Championed by 'media builder' Tommy Walsh, Dansand has a long lifespan, is weather resistant, environmentally friendly and harmless to children and animals.

A DODGY DICTUM?

We are removing several very large, old rhododendrons.
We have been told by several people that the bushes will
have poisoned the soil and that any replacement shrubs
we plant will die. Is this true?
Penelope, by email

I was asked a similar question at a talk I was giving in the
Surrey 'Rhododendron Belt'. (Well... why should it only be
Stockbrokers that have a Belt named after them?) Answering
as always off the cuff, i.e. not in a position to check any facts,
I gave an answer based on my own observations and
experience, which went as follows. Being wide-spreading and
often ground-huggingly low-growing evergreen shrubs,
rhododendrons create extremely dense canopies that
completely obliterate light under which their relatively
shallow roots sop up all the available moisture in the topsoil.
This combination of no light and minimal moisture makes it
impossible for other plants to survive under or around them.
Added to this, their long life ensures that their constantly
dropped, leathery leaves (that take literally years to rot down)
form a thick carpeting layer beneath them that makes seed
germination almost impossible. In my garden only the odd
tough laurel sapling gets beyond the seedling stage in the
gloom under my big rhodos. Some years ago I dug up and
gave away a few large ones (vibrantly puce-flowered... simply
couldn't stand them...). Before replanting the area with
gentler-toned things that would tolerate the dappled shade
and neutral/slightly acid prevailing soil (abelia, viburnums,
hydrangeas, daphnes and martagon lilies), I first removed and
binned the thick layer of un-rotted and half-rotted leaf litter,
improved the soil beneath it with my own compost and leaf
mould and added a little slow-acting bonemeal. Everything
thrives – giving no credence to the 'poisoned soil' theory.

However, after my Surrey experience I resolved to do more research online on what I have long believed to be a distinctly dodgy dictum – spread via word of mouth from generation to generation like a virus. I found that there was plenty written about all parts of rhododendrons being toxic to humans, but there was little proven science out there about them actually 'poisoning' soil. 🌿

SIZE (AND SEASONS) MATTER

Why are we told that when potting on pot-bound plants we should put them into containers only one size up from the one they are in, when if planted directly into the garden they would have unlimited root space?
Rose, Hereford

I agree, the advice does seem illogical, and ultimately somewhat extravagant (on pots, compost, time, etc), but there is some sensible science backing it up. Leigh Hunt at the RHS explains that it's not a completely hard-and-fast 'rule', but says the advice has a lot to do with moisture. A pot-bound plant becomes accustomed to coping without much of it, and also presumably accustomed (this is my own twopennyworth, not Leigh's) to the often-warm outer edges of its cramped living quarters. If suddenly transplanted into a large container full of evenly damp and probably cooler compost, the roots may simply start to rot.

The time of year you pot them on has a lot to do with it, too. Plants are less likely to suffer, more likely to snap into action, produce new roots and survive, if they are transferred from one pot to another in the growing season rather than when they are dormant in the winter.

As for plants going directly into the soil: this may explain why some things we plant in the autumn disappear without trace during their first winter. I admit to having had little disappointments in the past: so-called perennial, reliably drought-tolerant eryngiums, bought in rather cramped pots during a flight of fancy when in glorious husky silver-blue flower in July, planted out optimistically in October and never seen again. I am sure we have all done something similar. I should have potted them on and waited till the following spring before planting them – this is the advice I now always give about summer impulse-bought plants. 🌿

MOTHER'S DAY HYDRANGEAS

My children gave me a blue flowering hydrangea as a Mother's Day gift. The wee card included says it is an indoor plant. Is it truly an indoor-only plant? Will I not be able to plant it outside? If I do, would it need to come back in next winter?
Mary, Aberdeen

This ill-starred hydrangea is very definitely an outdoor plant. I have, in my time, seen numerous casualties of this sort: wizened little scrappits in plastic pots of desiccated multi-purpose compost reluctantly abandoned after many a dinner party/birthday/Mother's Day, etc.

The problem with what I rather dismissively call 'florist's' hydrangeas is that they have been forced into blooming at quite the wrong time, with the emphasis put on flower rather than root production. Their botanical clocks are all at sixes and sevens, and the effort and patience needed to get them back in the right time zone is quite reasonably considered by most of us to be a horticultural challenge too far.

12

What you should do with these exotic things is keep their roots just moist while they bloom. In due course, remove the faded flowers, cutting the stems down to a pair of leaves. After this the plants have to be kept just ticking over, somewhere light and really cool – they hate centrally heated conditions – until mid-May or thereabouts. Then they can be potted on into a larger pot of something suitable (50/50 loam-based John Innes No 3 and multi-purpose compost) and put outside in a fairly shady place for the hottest part of the summer while they recover their composure, growing leafy and even hopefully making a few new stems. Regular watering is important.

Get them into the ground in the autumn and they will have every chance of winter survival and may even flower a little the following summer. The next spring (my goodness this is beginning to sound like a real marathon… it is, but I have done it myself, so I know it works) they can be properly pruned and should go onwards and upwards.

Alternatively, bin the poor thing and have a kind but firm word with your children. ❧

A DUFF BATCH?

I bought two packets of nerine bulbs via mail order many months ago. I planted them in a south-facing position in two different gardens (seaside and country), both of them sheltered by brick walls. I have watered them regularly and surrounded them with compost. Alas they haven't grown up as expected. They are just a few inches in height and have no pink flowers yet. Did I get a duff batch?
Mary, by email

In the wilds of their native sunny South Africa, nerines grow in very poor, free-draining soil – the sort of situations that we can really only replicate at the base of south-facing walls in this country. The bulbs should be planted relatively shallowly – with the tops of their 'shoulders' exposed to the sun so they can bake a bit – in soil that has been opened up and made as free-draining as possible with the deep addition of grit. Established nerines produce their leaves during winter (once they have finished flowering around November), so the appearance of leaves on your new bulbs that have yet to flower is not unexpected. These need to get as much sun as possible, and will gradually yellow and fade away completely in the summer so that the startling stems of spidery, pink, lily flowers then appear as if out of nowhere. Nerines therefore look best grown where they can make thick rows or clumps. The variety that would have been sold to you is bound to be *Nerine bowdenii*, which is reliably hardy here. The compost mulch you applied will be useful frost protection for their first winter, but should be unnecessary thereafter.

I don't know what instructions accompanied your mail-ordered bulbs, but I would suggest that you were perhaps encouraged to be a little over-optimistic: given the right conditions, nerines should flower in their second year after planting. However, once they get going after year two, they should improve and reliably multiply year by year. ❧

SHADE GROUNDCOVER

In our new garden I should like to replace some untidy groundcover (an evergreen euphorbia) in front of a laurel hedge with some more interesting permanent flowering plants, but not shrubs. Can you suggest things that would grow in quite a bit of shade?
Sally, by email

The existing euphorbia (doubtless *E. amygdaloides* var. *robbiae*) is actually one of the best plants for the place you describe, and I suggest that you keep a clump or two, controlling it annually to maintain a 'balance of power' with softer herbaceous plants. This euphorbia is vastly improved if its spring-flowering shoots are cut right back once they have lost their lime-green brilliance.

You will need to improve the soil in the area with as much moisture-retaining organic matter as possible before replanting. You could go for simplicity by choosing an all-white colour scheme that would look bright and brilliant against the backdrop of so much permanent evergreen. The following is a list, starting with the tallest, of some of my personal favourites (all but one are perennials) that will cope with shade, given adequate moisture: *Anemone × hybrida* 'Honorine Jobert'; *Lunaria rediviva* (perennial honesty, actually very pale mauve); *Myrrhis odorata* (sweet cicely); *Lunaria annua* var. *albiflora* 'Alba Variegata' (biennial variegated white honesty); broadly striped thick-leaved (therefore more snail-proof) hostas and white-flowered Oriental hybrid hellebores. As gentle replacement groundcover you could try *Galium odoratum* (sweet woodruff), white-flowered *Cyclamen hederifolium* and *Milium effusum* 'Aureum' (Bowles's golden grass).

Don't forget, when you re-do this area, to leave a rough pathway along the back so that the hedge can be pruned annually. The soil there will be dry, full of roots and awful anyway, definitely a no-go area for herbaceous plants. ❧

A BOOK FOR PEDANTS LIKE ME

You may claim not to care sixpence about the conventional pronunciation of plant names, their origins and meaning, but if you have ever belonged to the Cotton Easter club, don't know if it is lissimakkia or lysimachia (and consequently mumble something in-between), if you stubbornly grow clemaytis when your snooty friends all grow clematis, take a look at *The A to Z of Plant Names* by Allen J Coombes (Timber Press). On about its third reincarnation, you can find it (of course) on Amazon.

CONTEMPLATING A TRICKY MOVE

I have a large and very vigorous plant of Himalayan honeysuckle that is rather too big for its allotted space. Ideally I would like to move it, but one that I moved in the past died on me. Is there a best time of year, or a particular knack to moving this plant?
Brenda, Market Deeping, Lincolnshire

This is one of those confusing plant names. To non-botanists, Himalayan honeysuckle bears little resemblance to the scented climbing honeysuckles with which we are more familiar, being a magnificent, upright, fast-growing plant with stout, hollow stems, blue-ish green foliage and, in late summer, 3in (7.5cm) pendent flower spikes with showy purple bracts. Shiny purple berries follow.

You are right, mature plants don't like being moved. You would perhaps do better to find a rogue seedling around the garden, pot it up and grow it on to plant out in autumn or the following spring in the place where you would like to move your existing plant. You are likely to find plenty of seedlings around since, if this plant has a fault, it is the fact that the birds adore the berries and the plant can actually become a bit of a weed if you let it.

In the meantime, to curb your frustration, you can prune your magnificent monster and thus substantially reduce its size. Since it flowers on new wood, you could remove at ground level with a slim pruning saw as many of the older shoots (the thickest and brownest) as you see fit. The youngest green shoots that grew from the base last year should be preserved intact unless they are too tall, in which case they can be halved along with the rest of the bush. Follow all this up with a feed and mulch, and you may even find that your slimmed-down shrub has earned a reprieve. ❧

DAHLIA DIVISION

*Having retrieved my dahlias from their winter hibernation
quarters (in a horse-feed trough at the back of my garage,
covered with straw and a blanket), thrown out those that
were soft and mushy and cleaned up and dried off those
that looked healthy, I am not sure what to do next. The
largest look as though they need splitting. How do you do
this? And a friend tells me I should get them growing in dry
compost before planting them. Is this right?*
Ian, by email

Everyone I know seems to do different things with dahlias –
it all depends on how cold it is where you live, whether you
grow them in containers, etc, etc. But you can split dahlias
quite easily by carefully cutting away some plump 'fingers'
from the bundle-y tubers. You have to make sure, however,
that each piece has a growing point at the top end (nearest to
the old stem), which may not be easy to detect when they are
totally dormant. So I suggest you do as your friend says:
separate some likely-looking pieces and start them off in some
dry (or at most barely moist) compost, before planting them
out when all danger of a sneaky night frost is over. This may
be as late as June in some parts. ❧

SCALE INSECTS

Wendy is wondering whether the nasty brown oval scale insects on her
loganberry are likely to also attack a nearby climbing hydrangea or
much-loved old rosemary bush. The answer is that it is unlikely. When

I last looked there were 16 different kinds of scale insects, each preferring to invade a different plant or family of plants. Some scale insects are just sandy beige, brown or black, oval or round, often quite tiny and hard to spot on stems and on the underside of leaves. The only evidence may be the black sooty deposit that develops on foliage, as a result of their excreta attracting mould spores. Other scale insects (amongst them *Eriococcus azaleae* which, as the name suggests, attacks plants in the azalea family) are more visible, particularly in spring when they are breeding, at which point each scale develops a distinct white waxy-woolly 'frill'. The treatment, however, is similar for all of them. Wendy is tackling her scale insects with neem oil and I suspect she will have an uphill battle. But where edible crops are not an issue, using a systemic insecticide early in the season when the young, more vulnerable 'nymphs' are on the move to feed off shoot tips is the best way of trying to beat or at least control an invasion – perhaps combined with disturbing the insects with a brush or with your hand.

THINGS TO CONSIDER IN MARCH

❋ Carefully remove the top few inches of compost from pots of lilies and replace with a 70/30 mixture of John Innes No 3 and leaf mould or multi-purpose compost.

❋ Don't be tempted to mow newly resurgent lawns too short. Neaten edges with shears. If they are really fuzzy after the winter, redefine them with a half-moon cutter.

❋ And don't be in too much of a hurry to start off seeds, particularly if you are a windowsill gardener. Later-sown seeds won't hang around getting leggy, and will inevitably 'catch up'.

❋ Bush roses pruned early are now producing lots of new buds. Carefully rub off any 'twins' you can see and also any inward-facing buds likely to become shoots that cross through the middle of the bush.

❋ Get a move on with planting new perennials and shrubs. The later they go in to the ground, the more fussing/watering you will have to do if we have a hot dry summer.

Secateurs and loppers at the ready

❋ Really tough, woody late summer-flowering shrubs can be cut back to a low woody framework now, and will make buds from old wood next month. Buddleja and *Hydrangea* 'Annabelle' fall into this category.

❋ Mop-head hydrangeas growing in mild situations can now have last year's flowering shoots cut back by a few inches (to a point just above fat buds), and oldest growth cut right out.

❋ Prune snow-damaged shoots from ornamental bay bushes using secateurs. Feed them with a general fertiliser.

❋ Cut back one in three branches of photinia to a point just above a leaf so that new red shoots will be produced just as the first crop fade to green.

❋ Penstemons will only flower on the new season's growth, so cut back their lofty leafy stems to within a few inches of the ground.

April

THINNING OUT, CUTTING BACK OR TRIMMING?
A 'hack-ology' guide for the perplexed

What exactly do we garden advisers mean by the various terms we use for pruning?

Suppose you have a fairly slow-growing *Viburnum × burkwoodii* that has kept its shape but gradually become too big for its allotted space. Books advise that it is best not to prune it, although it can be 'thinnned out' after flowering – but what exactly does that mean? Thinning out is all about encouraging new growth that will in due course flower better than the old stuff you have taken out. It is how you treat shrubs that flower on the previous year's shoots (philadelphus, ceanothus and so on), and is carried out immediately after flowering. Viburnum is a tricky one, however, and I had to tiptoe over my wet grass to look at my own specimen to work out the following. As it's an almost evergreen shrub that flowers on the tips of the previous season's fairly sparse growth, it would be a shame to limit its flower power by cutting it back too hard, so the job has to be done very gingerly after flowering (around May), every couple of years or so. One or two of the older, thicker branches that have flowered can be cut back by about half – to just above a pair of good buds. These will then sprout and produce growth that will eventually flower, but maybe not the following year. I would at the same time remove cleanly any skinny branches that are zipping off across the inside of the bush, in order to divert the shrub's energies into more productive growth.

And what of 'cutting back' – of shrubs that flower in late summer on the end of new growth? Buddlejas and short-lived lavateras (perhaps the most obvious examples) can be cut right back into old wood, controlling their size and improving their looks. They can be persuaded to produce flowers on staggered branches (if the plant is grown against a house or boundary, for example), by adjusting the height of the woody framework that remains after pruning. But with radical pruning jobs there are always complicated cases. Take the red-stemmed dogwood *Cornus alba*

'Sibirica', which needs to be cut back in spring in order to make it grow a new forest of scarlet stems. But if the shrub were to be cut back completely there would be a gaping hole in the border for months. This kind of dogwood really looks fabulous in winter if grown in groups in open, park-like gardens, where its complete demolition to ground level every April (as its red stems are about to leaf up) does not create 'holes'. So in a border, the answer is a compromise. Half the stems can be cut back to promote new bright stems. Those that remain can themselves be cut by half in mid-summer and will shoot again before the autumn. Result: red stems aplenty (lovely to use as exotic-looking, twiggy plant supports) and no 'holes'.

And 'trimming'? This is the dangerous one. 'Trimming' is what you do to small hedges – box and so on. (Potentilla is one of the few flowering shrubs that you can trim lightly each spring since it will flower its socks off all summer whatever you do to it.) On the whole, I think that gardens where all shrubs are regularly 'trimmed' look rather dreadful – we have all seen them: dense lollipops with congested woody interiors and precious few flowers. All it would need is a couple of Snickers wrappers and a Coke can or two, and you might think you were in a supermarket car park. Oooh, how nasty.

AILING MAGNOLIA

We are getting to the end of our tether with the ailing five-year-old specimen of **Magnolia** × soulangeana *planted in a prominent position in our garden. It flowers badly, its leaves turn brown at the tips during summer and it has not made much new growth. My husband wants to remove it, but has agreed I can keep it one more year if I can sort its problems out. Should I start by giving it an iron tonic?*
Jenni, by email

Magnolias tend to be happiest if they are grown in grass on their own, in slightly acid, cool, moist soil. You don't mention whether or not your tree is hemmed in between hot paving

22

stones, but if it is, it is unlikely to be happy. Nor do you mention whether or not the leaves of your magnolia are pale, which would indicate iron deficiency in the soil, but you should certainly check the pH (with a little kit available from garden centres). If it is high (indicating your soil is alkaline), a treatment with Sequestrene may be helpful – remember that after five years the magnolia's roots will have spread to quite a wide area. However, they also suffer if the soil around them lacks magnesium and this may be the main cause of the summer browning of your tree's leaf tips and general poor growth. This year, spray the leaves or water the ground around its roots with Epsom salts diluted in water (¾oz per 2 pints; 20g per litre) a couple of times during the growing season. The tree would also probably appreciate a dose of ericaceous shrub fertiliser and a hefty dollop of leaf mould this spring. Treated kindly thus it should reward you with a happier demeanour, better growth and, in due course, more flowers. I'll keep my fingers crossed. ❧

FELINE SURPRISED?

Wet weather is miserable for us all at any time of year – but particularly so for cats. Certainly you won't find them napping on the garden wall or lingering stoned and slitty-eyed around the catmint when the weather is foul. And with no favoured out-of-the-way dry and dusty bits to be found anywhere, when caught short they misbehave right in the middle of gravel paths, lawns – anywhere visible their tiny minds can think of, as if intent on making their displeasure as public as possible.

There is, however, great news from my friend Joan in Sussex who, pushed to the limit, decided to try out something I mentioned to her in passing some time ago; namely, a (relatively) benign way to curb feline excesses or at least send the blighters elsewhere to do their anti-social worst. I am happy to give a nod and smile of acknowledgement here to a fellow problem-solving garden writer, the very excellent and amusing Steve Bradley, from whom I got this tip originally. I have never had occasion to try it out myself, however, so I am grateful to Joan for having done so for me. This, dear readers, may well be the way forward for us all, as far as this particular problem is concerned.

Somewhere in your garden, where nothing else is currently growing, create a perfect seed bed, raking the soil to a fine tilth. As we all know, cats absolutely adore pristine bits of garden like this, considering them to have been created especially for them, for one purpose only.

Carefully dig a couple of holes in your immaculately prepared planting area, or even several holes if there is enough space, each about 12in (30cm) deep and wide. Inflate an equal number of balloons to their maximum and gently ease them into the holes you have dug, then fill in around them and very carefully re-rake the soil immaculately over the top so that the balloons are undetectable, just – but only just – below the soil surface. Those particularly enjoying this artful deception might even feel moved to indulge in a further bit of set dressing: to mark the spots with some labels traditionally embellished with seed packets, to indicate to your feline friends *exactly* where you have 'sown' things. (I shouldn't really need to add that you have to be careful where you tread at this point or the whole thing could end in disaster.) Sadly, the more malevolent amongst you might well think you will probably not have the pleasure of actually witnessing what happens next, but as sure as eggs is eggs, when the coast is clear, along will slink one of our furry friends with only one thing on his or her mind. Shortly after the start of that purposeful front-paw soft-shoe shuffle… well, I leave the rest to your imagination. Of course, no serious harm is done to the cat but – according to Joan – it really does put the wind up them.

ELDERLY CEANOTHUS

My ceanothus must be around 20 years old and stands about 6ft (1.8m) high – more like a small tree than a bush. The inner branches of the plant are dark and seem lifeless, and the leaves seem to be held only on the last 12in (30cm) or so of each branch and twig. It also seems to be loose in its foundations. Would really hard pruning revive it?
Marilyn, by email

At the ripe old age of 20, your ceanothus is on borrowed time. If you hard-prune it as you tentatively suggest, it will not shoot out from brown wood within, although it may produce some tiny sprouts from lower down on the trunk. If you are then tempted to cut it down – hoping the new sprouts become a new 'tree' – they won't, and the tree will most probably linger and die. If it is rocking on its roots that, too, indicates that it is not going to last much longer, whatever you do.

On a slightly more cheerful note: ceanothus is incredibly fast-growing, and one of the most instantly rewarding shrubs, along with the cistuses, to plant in a sunny, sheltered space. Replace your 'tree' with another, new and shrubby one, and from an early age prune it annually around this time of year, after it has finished flowering. You will be surprised how quickly it will grow. 🌿

PESKY PUPPY

Vikki wants to know what to feed her roses and other plants with now she has a new puppy. Previously she has alternated blood, fish and bone with chicken manure pellets, both of which seem to be irresistible to the silly thing. I think Vikki will have to use inorganic fertilisers for the foreseeable future: Miracle-Gro slow-release feeds might do the trick (there is now a rose and shrub one), or she could use good old-fashioned granular Growmore or equivalent.

IN LOVE WITH ANGELICA

Jane from Fordingbridge in Hampshire fell in love with a statuesque *Angelica gigas* plant in her friend's garden last year and has begged a small self-sown seedling from her, as well as some seed gathered from the same friend's garden previously. Jane's question: being a biennial, the young plant should flower this year, shouldn't it (even though it looks quite small)? And if she can get the seed to germinate now, will she have another young plant to take the place of the old one next year?

A loaded question, this one. Although it is often grown as such, this big green angelica is not a true biennial, but is better described as a monocarpic herbaceous perennial – which means it will make a handsome leafy plant for two or three, or possibly even four, years before flowering and setting millions of seeds, after which it will die. It will do this reliably if grown undisturbed in the ground from germination in ideal conditions and then thinned out, or if grown from seed in a pot, planted out in the spring when quite small and then left to its own devices. Importantly, angelica also needs moist soil to thrive and achieve its handsome, hefty stature. It sounds to me as if Jane's small plant is unlikely to flower this year, and it may even – the soil being rather dry this spring – suffer a real setback having had its roots disturbed. TLC will be of paramount importance this summer to ensure it makes a good root system in its new site.

As for the seed: angelica seed, like that of other plants in the umbellifer family, only germinates really reliably if it is very fresh. Jane

26

should sow plenty of seed to allow for the fact that she does not know how old it is. And bearing in mind all of the above, it is highly unlikely that the resulting plants will flower next year. They will still make lovely, jungly-looking plants though, so it is worth having a go.

THE RIGHT SUPPORT NETWORK

How do I cover a new and rather ugly east-facing 5ft (1.5m) high fence at the back of my garden? Having resisted planting a Russian vine, I have so far acquired a Clematis alpina *that's having a hard time trying to climb up a piece of trellis I provided for it. Have you any suggestions?*
Matt, by email

Covering fences quickly using assorted climbers is tricky if you want to avoid dreadful maintenance problems (i.e. a tangled mish-mash that is hard to prune) two or three years down the line. You could instead concentrate your efforts on growing a row of evergreen shrubs, some of which flower, some of which have interesting leaves or berries, to create a hedge that would quickly hide most of the fence and distract the eye away from it rather more successfully in the long term. Once these have got going you could then plant some small, non-rampant climbers (late-flowering clematis, perhaps, that are pruned down annually) or possibly even annual climbers that could all use the shrubs as climbing frames. Another possibility might be a hedge of mixed Rugosa roses – scented, disease free, with red hips the size of cherry tomatoes and brilliant golden yellow autumn foliage colour.

Clematis climbs by wrapping its leaf stems around anything it can find. As your delicate little alpina is finding, garden trellis is a bit too chunky for all but the most vigorous of clematises and you would do well to provide a finer mesh – criss-cross the trellis with fine wire, or bang some coarse chicken wire on to it. ❦

URBAN WORM POWER

*I have a London flat with two large balconies, one each
side of the building, both of which get useful amounts
of sun. I really want to have a small compost heap since
I rather object to throwing away vegetable waste that
could be converted into something useful for my plants.
How can I go about composting on such a small scale?*
Matthew, by email

Composting on a really small scale is tricky – to be successful
you need a certain amount of bulk to get the rotting process
going, and of course, a balanced mixture of dry/green waste.
All that cold, wet kitchen/vegetable waste in a conventional
compost bin would just sit there and start to smell.

What I feel you need is an army of little red chaps to help
you out. Have you thought about installing a wormery on one
of the balconies? These are excellent for processing kitchen
vegetable waste without any nasty smells, and they also
absorb a useful amount of shredded paper, as well as any
snippings and trimmings from your balcony plants. In brief,
after a few months of 'feeding' the wormery, you would get a
small amount of very sludgy odour-free compost (excellent for
adding to your own potting composts), as well as being able
to draw off (via a tap) lots of concentrated brown liquid
fertiliser that can be bottled and stored, and diluted 1 part
to 10 with water to feed all your balcony plants. Placed
somewhere neither too sunny nor too cold, the worms would
doubtless be very active most of the year round because of the
natural shelter provided by your balcony. I write with great
enthusiasm about this because I have had a wormery by my
back door for more years than I care to think about,

specifically for kitchen waste and shredded paper. No smell, no trouble. In my case the sludge gets used as an accelerator for my regular garden compost bins. ❦

DIPS IN THE LAWN

Over the years our lawn has developed shallow dips and hollows that we now need to fill. It will take a lot of lawn sand to do it. Can we use washed sand from a builders' merchant for this purpose?
Christopher, by email

'Lawn sand' is the name given to a traditional sand-based lawn treatment that contains iron sulphate and ammonium sulphate and generally peps up the condition of a poor lawn. When applied (in spring or early summer), the sand settles on the moss and on the broad-leaved weeds (which the iron sulphate then kills, turning badly infested areas of the lawn temporarily black), but it rather niftily slides off the narrow, more vertical leaves of the grass, which is 'greened up' by the ammonium sulphate. The sand, meanwhile, goes some way to improving the texture of the soil and helps with drainage. Lawn sand is not, however, something you would chuck over a bumpy lawn on a regular basis to iron it out.

You could indeed use washed sand (not regular builders' sand), but ideally what you need is in fact called 'turf dressing' or 'lawn top dressing', which is increasingly hard to find in bags at garden centres – you may need to look on the internet for bulk suppliers (such as Gardenscape Direct in the south-east). This top dressing, traditionally containing sand and peat, now generally consists of a mixture of sand and a loam-based compost. Some gardeners mix up their own, using sand and sieved, moisture-retaining home-made compost or leaf mould. For a badly draining lawn, you would use a mixture that is heavy on the sand; for a droughty lawn, one that is heavy on the moisture-retaining materials. By brushing a very thin layer over the lawn each year you can gradually improve the quality of the soil and reduce drainage problems, and also level out, to a certain extent, slight hollows. Too thick a layer of turf dressing can actually kill the grass, though – so deep hollows would have to be dealt with differently, by carefully peeling back the turf and adding an appropriate layer of garden soil to smooth out the hollow before treading the turf gently back into place. 🌿

GROWING BASIL

I have a lot of trouble growing basil in my herb garden.
Have you any tips?
Tom, by email

Basil, I find, is one of those herbs that germinates easily – in which case you have a glut – or not at all, and then you end up buying pots of it from the supermarket. It has to be started off under glass, only thriving outside in our climate from mid-June onwards, when it has a tendency to go to seed fast unless the shoot tips are pinched out regularly, and is all too frequently prey to whitefly.

A word about supermarket basil: close examination of the pots will reveal that they contain a host of little seedlings. If you pull these out very gently one by one when you need basil for cooking, instead of just pulling off leaves or cutting the tops off shoots, you will be left with one or two small plants that can then be potted on into a bigger container with some John Innes No 2 compost and grown properly – preferably outside in a sunny patch. Don't try to separate these last stalwarts or disturb them unduly during the re-potting process, however, or they may give up on you.

You can propagate basil by sticking cut stems in a jar of water. Roots appear on them within a week or so and if you are careful you can pot them up and grow them on. Pinch out the tips of each to make them bush up a bit.

And if you do have a glut of basil, turn to June, page 71, for instructions on making herb oils. 🌿

DRAMA FOR A BIG POT

In the summer my paved and fairly sunny area is occupied by a large table and chairs. To give me something to look at while these are stored for the winter, I have acquired a very large frost-resistant terracotta pot (not so large that it can't be moved out of the way in the summer) and wonder if you could suggest what I should put in it that would be interesting in winter/spring.
Linda, East Yorkshire

I feel that all this pot needs to make a statement is to be kept really simple, with a single shrub on its own, rather than crammed with too many things – which would put everything under pressure and could look rather itsy-bitsy (sorry, but 'itsy-bitsy' is really the most appropriate term I can come up with). My mind immediately envisaged a magnificent prostrate rosemary spilling out of this pot. Rosemary, either in the form of 'Miss Jessopp's Upright' or slumpy varieties such as the dark-flowered 'Fota Blue', can always be used to add evergreen structure here and there in the sunnier parts of a garden, flowering really early (April/May) and then smelling wonderful every time you brush past the leaves. It also looks exceptionally 'at home' in terracotta pots, I think.

Raise the pot off the ground on bricks, which will get rid of the need for loads of crocks in the bottom of the pot and leave more space for the shrub's roots: rosemary hates waterlogged roots. Or, instead of bricks, you could consider keeping it on a little wheeled wooden platform such as you find for sale in some garden centres. This would make it easier to shunt the pot about as necessary. You would also do well to line the pot with plastic (adapt the bottom of an old compost bag, cutting a hole in the bottom – but make sure it doesn't show at the top). Terracotta, being porous, can dry out inconveniently often in hot or windy weather. ❧

MINI-MEADOWS

I decided to leave the corner of my garden under a young cherry tree for wildlife, so I sowed poppies and cornflowers, which flowered quite happily last year. But now the grass has romped away and the whole area is a mess. Should I thin the grass out or is there a way to mow this sort of area without losing the interesting flowering plants?
Jakki, Cheshire

Sowing a few wildflower seeds in a small area and hoping they will form the basis of a pretty self-managing mini-meadow is a bit of a pipe dream – and one upon which I hate to pour cold water, but (very aware of the curiously mixed metaphor) pour just a little cold water on it I should. The poppies and cornflowers were destined only to last for a year, since they are cornfield annuals that do better in frequently disturbed ground, finding it hard to compete with grass.

You might have more success with some meadow perennials. You will be able to get small plants of wildflowers around now from many of the more clued-up garden centres. Before you plant them, however, mow the grass extremely short (and pick up all the bits) in order to minimise competition. Easy perennials to start with are various campions, ox-eye daisy and knapweed, all of which will carry flowers well above the level of the grass and will eventually seed around. They can also cope with being mown short (along with the grass), towards the end of the summer, through the autumn and on into the spring. At this point (around late April) you should stop mowing, and let everything grow and flower – hey presto, a pretty, summer-flowering mini-meadow that lasts about two months or so.

The other kind of mini-meadow would be a purely spring-flowering one, with fritillaries, little daffodils, cowslips, primroses and so on. This kind you absolutely can't mow in spring and furthermore you have to leave the area rather unkempt and unattractive through the early part of the summer until bulb leaves have died away. Then the grass can be mown fairly regularly until late autumn and even in winter as necessary.

I should add as a general postscript that, fun though they are, whatever type of wildflower area you decide to create there will be lengthy periods when there is nothing going on in it, and other times when it will be – how shall I put it – downright unsightly. The books that tempt us don't show you those bits, though. ❦

DEER, DEER…

…Deer, loads of them in broad daylight in our new three-quarter-acre (third of a hectare) hedged garden. At first, we were enthralled by them – even crept around the house peering at them, trying not to disturb them. Then we started to make a garden and realised what we were up against. We are about to try to establish a clematis walkway, which presumably stands no chance, and, amongst other grand plans, aim to plant a lavender hedge up the drive – presumably ditto. What can we do?
Jacky, by email

There are some deer-proof plants, but not enough of them (a helpful list is to be found on the RHS website, rhs.org.uk). But I think honestly that you are going to have to throw money at this and in my view it would be totally disheartening to implement any really grandiose horticultural plans until you have done so. Initially you will need to put up a tall wire fence within your boundary, and then plant a second hedge next to it that will eventually disguise the wire. The theory is that deer will leap over or bluster through a single hedge but they are much more cautious when faced with two hedges with a substantial gap between or better still a hedge/wire/hedge combination.

If that sounds like a frighteningly expensive no-no, here is a brief rundown of 'deterrents' suggested by readers. There is a product called Grazers that they don't like (the deer, not the readers, although some of the latter are highly sceptical) but which needs repeat applications every four weeks or so; a radio in a plastic bag, constantly tuned to Radio 5 (i.e. a scary voice station rather than soothing pastoral music) that you move around un-nerves them. Grated soap, rags or rope barriers soaked in various malodorous cleansing products and bags of hair (begged from hairdressers) strung around the place all meet with mixed success. And apparently, says a reader, deer are frightened of rustling plastic shopping bags hanging along boundaries and will steer clear of them – this bit is absolutely true, if somewhat unsightly. But definitely the most effective kind, she said, presumably with tongue firmly in cheek, are those provided by a certain supermarket because they are known to Always Scare Deer Away. ❧

THINGS TO CONSIDER IN APRIL

❋ Deadhead daffodils as they finish flowering (removing the stems as well or they stick up untidily when the leaves collapse).

❋ Review your needs with regard to plant supports. Metal hoops and grids of all sorts do a good job, last for years and are unobtrusive.

❋ Pick off and squash scarlet lily beetles, newly emerged from underground hibernation and feasting on fritillaries and other lily relatives. If you use insecticides, spray growing lily shoots with systemic Provado Ultimate Bug Killer Ready to Use as a precaution.

❋ Mowing starts in earnest this month. Grass seed will also germinate quickly from now on, so repairs and patches will 'heal' fast.

❋ Inspect lidded plastic compost bins and also stir the contents. If it all seems a bit too wet in there, leave the lid off for a few hours and add some shredded paper or cardboard.

April annual weed wars – hoe, dig or pull?
❋ Only use a hoe on weed seedlings on sunny days when the soil is dry. Otherwise disturbed weedlings may re-root and go on growing.

❋ While hairy bittercress is easy to pull out, top growth of established fine-rooted weeds like chickweed or goose grass will snap and the plants will re-grow. Don't use a hoe – use two hands. Grab the top growth and loosen the roots with a hand fork in order to pull up whole plants.

❋ Don't compost annual weeds. Some may already carry ripening seeds.

❋ It really is true. Let your weeds go to seed one year, and you will be weeding for the next seven. That's how long seeds can linger in topsoil.

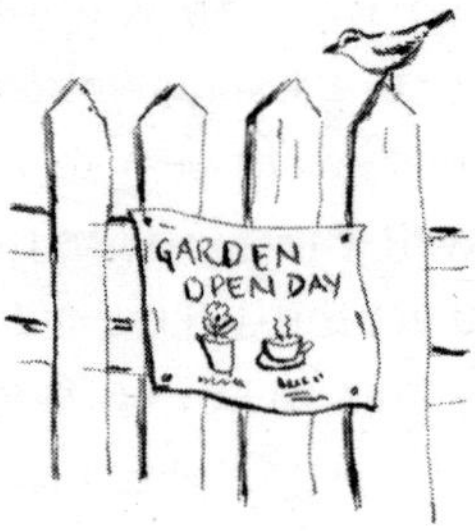
GARDEN
OPEN DAY

May

GARDEN OPENING

Letting people in to have a look at your garden is not really about showing off in the ordinary sense – it is just as much about sharing what you see and marvel at on a daily basis. Some, although maybe not all, of your visitors will absolutely 'get' what you are up to and say so, which will give you a real shot in the arm. Of course there are some other less comfortable aspects: you will always have the odd competitive gardener turn up who may murmur darkly about their own garden being much 'better' than yours, those who seem to be there on a weed-spotting mission and inevitably, if you go to the trouble of offering such now-expected luxuries, you get the determined tea-and-cake munchers, the worst of whom barely raise their eyes from the trough to look at the garden.

Sadly, I rarely find time to see as many other gardens as I would like to, neither those open occasionally for charity nor those of the Great and Good that are open regularly. When I do manage to escape and look at gardens, large or small, I am invariably bowled over by some aspect or other of them and return home with fresh ideas and insights. This is why I urge others to visit gardens and to open their own. It can be an energising learning experience, quite apart from the enjoyment factor.

Your garden does not have to be large, posh or unusual to be of interest to others. Everyone who gardens knows the score – that we all have to fight the same battles. I dug around in my Thorny Problems archive and turned up the following advice I handed out to a couple of nervous garden owners in the spring before they opened their garden for one afternoon in May.

Whatever you do, it is really important, I feel, that you don't let an event like this – just one afternoon in your gardening year – take over your life. And, tempting though it may be, don't replant your garden so that it will look 'special' on the day: the last thing people want to see is a load of ill-at-ease garish annuals splattered around the place in an attempt to make the garden look colourful and stuffed. However, there are some ways in which you should think ahead. As spring progresses, make sure that you put your herbaceous plant supports in place in good time so that you are not wading through borders, shoring things up, the day before your opening. And do deadhead everything for a good fortnight before the big day and make sure the lawn looks tidy. To avoid embarrassment, learn the names of most of your plants because people will ask you – although in my experience there is always some smarty-pants around who will delight in prompting/correcting you if sheer nervous exhaustion overcomes you when put on the spot.

Lastly, remember that you are not preparing for an exam in best horticultural practice: people will get a lot of pleasure simply soaking up the individual atmosphere of your garden, happy to pick up some good ideas while contributing to charity. Above all, lap up all the appreciation – enjoy your day.

KILLER CLEMATIS?

Michael asks if the *Clematis montana* 'Rubens Superba' that he planted seven years ago to climb his apple tree – and which now has made an umbrella of growth over it – will eventually kill the tree, as he has been warned. It will certainly mess up its growth and thus eventually weaken its fruiting performance. I always think apple trees make disappointing hosts for *Clematis montana* – since they both flower very pale-pinkly at virtually the same time, thereby visually cancelling each other out.

IMPATIENCE NOT REWARDED

Terry's two-year-old evergreen climbing *Hydrangea seemannii*, well fed and looking healthy, is three feet up a north-facing wall but refuses to flower. Has he been sold a pup, he asks? I doubt it very much – it just needs more time. Probably as much as another two or three years. Patience is called for, I feel.

ALLIUMS IN POTS?

I am new to gardening. I fell for some purple-flowered alliums – 'Purple Sensation' – and decided to plant them in a container in my small courtyard garden. They have grown well and are about to flower, but the leaves are extremely messy and starting to turn yellow. Can I cut them off?
Sandy, by email

The mess is relatively short-lived, and I wouldn't cut the leaves back while they are still green. Allium leaves can be removed once they have turned bright yellow, around the time they start to flower. The flowers will then set seed in splendid isolation and eventually dry off rather beautifully.

The last thing I would want to do is put you off experimenting with plants, but I suggest that alliums are not a particularly good subject to plant all on their own in a container in a small garden for the very reason you mention – their leaves are hard to live with. These and other alliums look rather better if they can be planted with something else in front of them that will hide their undercarriage in its brief ugly phase. In my garden I grow big purple alliums in amongst a colony of biennial white-flowered honesty (a plant that has similarly attractive dried seed heads). The allium buds are now just appearing over the froth of white flowers that disguises the allium foliage. The honesty will be selectively edited as it finishes flowering to allow the alliums more prominence. The remaining honesty and the alliums will then be allowed to dry off together.

If you can't find a space in your small garden where you can transfer your alliums to the ground (in September, in a sunny spot that has well-drained soil), with something taller in front of them to hide their spring foliage, then organising your containers into a group with something shrubby to do a similar job in spring might be the answer. If you are a 'formal' gardener, try them in a small troupe of potted box balls; if you aren't, then hiding them amongst temporarily filled raggedy pots of wallflowers might do the trick. ❧

JAPANESE KNOTWEED

The surveyor of our proposed new property has suggested that there might be Japanese knotweed in one section of the garden. How difficult is it to eradicate or control?
Roger, Worthing, West Sussex

It is difficult to be specific on this one, since it is probably still too early in the year to assess just how extensive this potentially horrid problem is going to be, and you and your surveyor may not be able to tell if the section of the garden is just the tip of a very large local iceberg. You could ask owners of neighbouring properties just how bad the problem is for them.

Japanese knotweed is one of the most dreaded of garden weeds. It produces each year numerous stout, hollow shoots around 6½ft (2m) in height from huge, almost indestructible, underground spreading roots. Under the Wildlife and Countryside Act 1981 you must not intentionally plant invasive species such as knotweed and neither must you allow them to spread on to adjacent land.

You will have an extremely hard job eradicating it, particularly if it is on the boundary of your proposed property – i.e. if you do not have total access to the whole plant.

The Environment Agency has produced a guide, for

developers rather than gardeners – but it still makes useful reading. As with tackling many tough weeds, they suggest it's best to wait before applying a herbicide: spring applications are less effective. Glyphosate is a good choice as it's systemic and spreads right through the plant. Treat knotweed between July and September – it's even worth pouring glyphosate down the cut hollow stems – but be prepared to wait up to three years before it stops growing back. Even then the rhizome may be dormant, lurking unseen – simply disturbing the soil nearby may stimulate it back into life.

Those unfortunate enough to suffer from this weed in their gardens also endeavour to control it after a fashion by mowing it regularly and by using flame throwers. However, if your property is bordered by grass verges treated by the local council, who have far stronger weedkillers at their disposal than we ordinary gardening mortals do, then there is a chance that between you, you would be able to get the upper hand. 🌿

LOOKING AFTER GRASSES

Rosemary from Bristol is with great difficulty trying to lift and divide a large *Miscanthus* 'Silberfeder' that has become too big for its boots. She remembers reading something about some grasses being better divided/planted in spring and others in autumn. How can you tell which need what and when?

There seems to be fairly widespread confusion about grasses, and botanists have helpfully shuffled them into two basic groups according to their climatic origins, which sorts out the maintenance nicely.

Grasses from cool climates include carex, calamagrostis, chasmanthium, deschampsia, festuca, hakonechloa, helictotrichon, molinia and stipa. They need to be divided every three years or so, or they lose their vigour; and in between times they benefit from a good 'groom' – cutting down old flower stems and tatty leaves in late winter or early spring just before they come into growth (often I comb out the dead stuff with a fine-tined shrub rake used upside down, but with the more robust grasses you can simply shear everything away). Some of these grasses have very recognisable seedlings and, rather than split the parent plant, I just earmark one or two seedlings and transplant them to replace their elderly parents every so often.

Grasses from warm climates include arundo, cortaderia (pampas grass), imperata, miscanthus, panicum, pennisetum, phalaris and spartina. They really don't need to be divided often unless, like the *Miscanthus* 'Silberfeder', they become seriously dense and bulky (which can be a problem in small gardens). These grasses are perhaps less robust than the cool climate grasses and don't really get going until late spring. They do best if they are divided when the soil is starting to warm up, around now. Plants that are left in situ and not divided should have some of their top growth left to provide just a bit of winter protection. This can be shortened very carefully as the new fresh growth puts in an appearance in late spring.

OF CHELSEA CHOPPING

Jane from Chichester asks whether she can bring forward the 'Chelsea chop' as her garden is more advanced than usual. The Chelsea chop, for the uninitiated, is a technique normally employed around Chelsea Flower Show time at the end of May (hence the name), whereby you manipulate various herbaceous plants by shortening some or all of their stems by up to a half, just before they form their flower buds. This causes them to have a bit of a hiccup, but subsequently makes them flower a little later on slightly stockier, branched stems, with more – but often smaller – blooms. What happens if you do this earlier depends entirely on the weather. Without any meaningful rain, for example, at worst, I suspect the plants will flower quite intensely, rather too briefly and a couple of weeks later than they would have done if left alone, but on abnormally short stems. Well, whatever... that's gardening for you... every year is different... (see also July, page 86).

DUSTBOWL PLANTING

Janet from Sudbury is a bit behind with things and wonders if she dare plant anything new in her dustbowl of a garden. Yes, Janet, go on, dare. This is how I go about it when the soil is dry and rain isn't imminently forecast. Dig your planting holes, incorporate plenty of organic matter in the soil around and about, fill the hole with water and let it drain away... twice. Then plant as usual, having dunked the new plants in a bucket of water till the air bubbles stop coming out of their compost. Water the plants into their new (already thus damp) homes, but lightly, just to settle them. Then firm them in gently and earth up with the surrounding dry soil/compost mix. Resist the temptation to water them again for a week or two. The plants will start to put their roots down (not up) and the dry soil on top will keep things moist below while they do so.

RUSTY ROSES

I have two roses, 'New Dawn' and 'Louise Odier' with, respectively, Clematis *'Étoile Violette' and* C. × durandii *growing through them, making lovely combinations. For the past couple of years, however, the roses have developed rust. Is there anything I can do to prevent this recurring?*
Marian, by email

Rose rust, which shows up in spring as orange dusty spores on stems and new leaves, is a parasitic fungal disease that is specific to roses (i.e. it will not spread to other garden plants). As the season progresses, the orange spores on the backs of infected leaves turn black, and the leaves start to drop prematurely. Badly affected roses gradually deteriorate. One course of action that should help (although it is a little late this year) is to clear away all fallen leaves so that the spores do not linger. You could prune out the worst-affected shoots as well, and keep the plants well fed and watered, so that their

43

growth remains as vigorous as possible and can fight off the fungus. This general TLC, including thick mulching in spring, will benefit both the roses and the clematis.

It does sound from your description as though your roses are unusually hard hit, and that it might be best to use a spray. Chemical sprays that are systemic such as Systhane Fungus Fighter or FungusClear Ultra by Scotts, used as the roses start to make their leaf buds, may act as a preventative. ❦

LAVENDER PEST

Every year in early summer, my lavender bushes become infected with blobs of white foam ('cuckoo spit'), each containing one to three tiny bugs. They are bright green and quite lively. Are these harmful and what might they turn into, as I've never witnessed the end result?
Pauline, by email

The 'lively' little green bug-eyed inhabitants of the tiny dollops of froth that can festoon the likes of lavender and rosemary are the nymphs of a sap-sucking common froghopper (*Philaenus spumarius*). The female hoppers lay eggs on the backs of leaves in autumn, which then overwinter and hatch out in early May, the nymphs rapidly covering themselves with a foam that they excrete from their backsides, which acts as a protection against predators – including somewhat hopeful gardeners who imagine that it might be possible to get rid of the problem with a garden hose.

A systemic insecticide sprayed on the bushes in early May will help to nip the froghopper/cuckoo spit problem in the bud, so to speak, but the frothy dots around the affected shrubs soon disappear and the activity of adult froghoppers causes little disastrous damage in a flower garden. If you still want to get rid of them and dislike the idea of using chemicals, you could call upon the services of junior gardeners. Children are remarkably good at froghopper control, since in my experience many of them take an utterly revolting delight in delving into the froth with thumb and forefinger, triumphantly capturing the lunching, munching nymphs and immediately squashing them. I've seen grown-ups do it too. ❦

IT'S 'ALL TOO GREEN'

The month of May in Belinda's garden is all too green, she complains. The daffodils and snowdrops are long gone, tulips don't like her soil so she only grows them in pots, forget-me-nots always get mildew so she has given them up, and she also avoids wallflowers because they go on and on, messing up her summer plans involving annuals that won't do much until July anyway. And such perennials as she has – campanulas and daisies – are all June/July performers. Have I any suggestions for plants that will give her a more colourful May next year, she asks?

I hardly know where to start with this tale of woe, since I actually relish the bursting-forth, full-of-promise greenness of May. I went for a prowl around my own square-footage to gather inspiration for a morale-boosting May List for Belinda.

For a start, green is itself a glorious colour, and one of infinite variation: the shade-loving limey biennial *Smyrnium perfoliatum* is one of the stars of May; as are loads of euphorbias (*E. polychroma, E. rigida, E. characias* subsp. *wulfenii, E. amygdaloides, E. mellifera*…). Here and there are soft, bright tussocks of Bowles's golden grass, cushions of golden feverfew, tufts of juvenile golden marjoram. Further back in the borders are the numerous green-ish upright flower wands of *Tellima grandiflora*, while the acid foliage of *Geranium* 'Ann Folkard' is already starting its scrambly growth towards its favourite summertime host, grey-leaved *Nepeta* 'Walker's Low'. On the subject of foliage, let's not forget contrasts of texture: the feathery burgeoning growth of nigella or fennel, new leaves of lady's mantle, each with a pearly raindrop sitting in its lap, and the fleshy other-worldly foliage of big border sedums. And buds: the fat drumsticks of tall alliums make a huge green statement well before they open.

Creamy-white flowers have taken over from the yellows of spring: sweet cicely is in flower, as are Solomon's seal and lily of the valley; drifts of white honesty and of gently invasive sweet woodruff, making inroads into the shade under shrubs. In a rough grassy area where fritillaries are just departing, pink campion is arriving, and tall, dark and handsome camassias are just opening up their starry blue flowers. Several different early-flowering rosemaries give me more blues and greys, while loads of spotty-leaved blue/pink pulmonarias have been buzzing with bees all month. All of these and more, many of them perennials, have been rioting away in my own small garden in May. And I haven't even mentioned the shrubs...

AEONIUM CARE AND PROPAGATION

I have two Aeonium *'Zwartkop'. They are kept indoors in winter, put outside in summer, and only watered when their compost is completely dry. One is branched and over 4ft (1.2m) tall, the other is single stemmed and slightly shorter. They were re-potted last year and while they are looking reasonably good, their lower leaves keep shrivelling and dropping. Am I not watering them correctly? And how can I propagate from one or both of them?*
Jo, by email

These aeoniums, both the green and the 'black' ('Zwartkop') ones, are handsome and tender succulents with quite special needs. Loads of us seem to fall for them in the summer and (unlike you, who seem to have triumphed, I hasten to say) manage to kill them in the winter.

First the shrivelling of lower leaves. This, although slightly annoying, is entirely normal as the plant makes a great spurt of growth upwards in spring. At the same time the colour of the rosettes of 'Zwartkop' seem to become a more vibrant dark purple, having become somewhat greenish in the low light of winter. The watering regime you describe is fine: compost for succulents should be loam-based, really gritty and therefore extremely free-draining. Weighty but porous terracotta pots make these potentially top-heavy aeoniums more stable.

As for propagation, I would leave the branched plant (which sounds rather fabulous) alone this year. The single-stemmed plant, being presumably a bit of an ugly duckling, is absolutely perfect material for you to try your hand at propagation. Cleanly cut the stem a few inches below the rosette, let its cut surface dry out for a week (to stop it rotting), before firming it gently into a 50/50 mixture of barely moist, loam-based cutting compost (John Innes No 1) and coarse sand. It should root within three or four weeks, and can be eventually potted on into the gritty compost mixture you used before. The stem of the decapitated remainder of the plant can be shortened considerably (you can simply bin the bit of naked stem that you remove) and should spontaneously sprout in several places, creating another branched plant. You can propagate from some of these, too, in due course, to form even more plants. Et voilà, from one ugly duckling, multiple beautiful black swans. 🌿

NATURALISING FRITILLARIES

Joyce wants the snakeshead fritillaries (*Fritillaria meleagris*) in her orchard to naturalise extensively and wonders if this will be best achieved if she removes the seed heads that are swelling up now, as she does with her daffodils, in order to encourage the bulbs to put energy into the production of next year's flowers. Fritillaries naturalise rather well if they are growing in the right (cool, moist-soiled) spot in rough grass that is only occasionally mowed. In the past I have found that simply helping nature along a bit has achieved relatively quick results. I allowed seed to ripen, let some drop naturally and then broadcast more by hand in suitable areas once the grass had been given its annual short cut in mid to late summer. Newly germinated seedlings are as skinny as blades of grass and don't make flowering-sized bulbs for a year or three. The parent bulbs, meanwhile, will also expand and flower better each year, largely unaffected by the fact that they have produced masses of seed.

BAY REPLACEMENT

Having lost one lollipop bay tree after another in two successive cold winters, I am now looking for a hardier replacement plant as the central focal point of my herb garden. Would an olive tree be any more hardy than bay? The plot is against a west-facing fence and is fairly sheltered. Have you any suggestions?
Patricia, by email

I think you are right to hesitate before opting for an olive tree. Having lost two bays, it would seem that this is actually rather a cold spot despite the fence, and an even more tender olive would probably fare no better. Incidentally, with these tender trees, it is the slim trunk that is particularly vulnerable and needs serious protection. If that freezes through for any length of time, the tree dies. (Mimosa is another one – I get a lot of letters about that, too.)

If the drainage of your soil is perfect, you could try planting an upright rosemary ('Miss Jessopp's Upright') and train/prune it into a series of irregular spires, which would look good in what seems to be a fairly formal setting. Holly is as tough as old boots, and you can buy little trained 'lollipop' trees of this or of Portugal laurel (*Prunus lusitanica*), the variegated versions of both being less vigorous than the green ones. Another idea is that you give up the 'statement plant' and go for a smart urn or Mediterranean pot as a centrepiece. 🌿

WEEPING WILLOW

The young weeping willow tree we planted by a natural pond in our garden has become rather sick. In early summer some of its leaves go yellow and spotty and drop off. Later in the summer it seems to recover, and by the autumn all seems well although the tree's general growth is rather less beautiful than it should be. I have loved weeping willows since my childhood – for me it is a 'must have' tree. What can we do to improve its general health?
Marcia, by email

Your tree is suffering from a fungal disease known as willow anthracnose that is almost impossible to cure. When I investigated this problem in the past, I was advised that treatment with a fungicide (even if the trees are small enough to spray) is unlikely to be of any use in controlling the disease since the fungus (*Marssonina salicicola*) overwinters in the lesions on the damaged shoots and very probably in the fallen leaves around the tree.

If the leaf fall becomes too irritating and the tree becomes an eyesore, you may decide to cut your losses while it is young and even start again with a new one. There are some cultivars that are more resistant than others to willow anthracnose and I would suggest you go to seek them out at a specialist tree nursery where they are used to dealing with whole mouthfuls of repetitive Latin. You should avoid, for example, *Salix* × *sepulcralis* var. *chrysocoma* (which is probably the variety you have) and instead seek out *Salix babylonica* var. *pekinensis* 'Pendula', which is reputedly far less likely to succumb. 🌿

FIVE TIPS FOR IRRITABLE HARD-PRESSED GARDENERS

1. Keep a large plastic plant pot by the compost bin in which to sling old plant labels, ties and assorted plastic detritus that could otherwise annoyingly end up back in the borders.

2. Two pairs of machine-washable stretchy nitrile gardening gloves are essential. One to wash, one to wear. Gardening without is unthinkable.

3. Essential pocket-kit for even the briefest trip round the garden: pair of old kitchen scissors, scraps of re-usable Flexi-Tie and a paper hankie. All will be needed within the first half an hour.

4. To save time and much small-print squinting: copy printed dilution rates of soluble feeds, pesticides, fungicides, etc and pin the list on the inside of the shed door. Clued-up gardeners will of course have saved them on their smartphones.

5. Keep your smartphone in the back pocket of your jeans, not the breast pocket of your shirt. Especially important, this one, for owners of garden ponds.

NEONICOTINOIDS – KEEPING UP IS HARD TO DO

There is much anxiety amongst those gardeners who still use systemic chemicals (maybe as a last resort) for the control of garden pests. Has the EU decided to ban all pesticides containing neonicotinoids, now apparently proved to be devastating to the bee population, for ever? Despite the dramatic headlines, the whole matter is not as cut and dried as it would seem. At the moment, only systemic products that contain the chemicals clothianidin, imidacloprid or thiamethoxam have been withdrawn from the shelves. And it is now illegal to use any old stock you may have hanging around. This should be disposed of through your local waste authority – usually your local household waste recycling centre, but check first.

Provado Lawn Grub Killer (imidacloprid) from Bayer is likely to be the one that most gardeners might miss, but there is of course a biological control (Nemasys Chafer Grub Killer) that will do the job. Bayer changed their other systemic insecticides some time ago. Without exception they all now contain thiacloprid, one of the next generation of neonicotinoids, not named on the recent hit list and thought to have a good profile for bees. Apart from Provado Ultimate Bug Killer Ready to Use, Multirose Bug Killer and Baby Bio House Plant Insecticide, familiar names now have the number 2 after their name: thus Provado Ultimate Bug Killer 2, Provado Vine Weevil Killer 2, etc. The equally well-known BugClear products from Scotts contain yet another (not yet banned) second-generation neonicotinoid called acetamiprid.

And a final word comes from Guy Barter, chief horticultural advisor at the RHS, with whom I had a general chat about pesticides. The RHS urges gardeners to use even the currently 'un-banned' systemic insecticides with sensitivity and caution, following package instructions to the letter and spraying at dusk, preferably when plants are actually seen to be damaged by insect attacks and never, of course, when they are in flower.

WEED SEEDS

Emailer Roma has noticed with some alarm that the dandelion heads that in her haste she just snips off and leaves on the ground go on and try to become 'clocks'. Are the seeds from these viable? Should she therefore be picking up the lopped flower heads? Yes to both questions. The flowers of all dandelion relations (groundsel, etc) and many other weeds with blowy seeds can go on maturing, so it is best to drop them in a bucket of water or bin them. An idea for Roma: a little dab of Roundup Weedkiller Gel where it hurts would see the dandelions off for ever, leaving her more time for other gardening pursuits.

Well, not quite...

CLOCKING OFF?

I was interested in your comments on dandelion seeds in which you advised Roma to drop them in a bucket of water. Wouldn't composting them be a sensible idea? Would the seeds not eventually be destroyed there? As my garden borders an agricultural grazing field, I am also concerned with thistle seeds and dock seeds. Can a compost heap destroy these as well? Dock seeds seem particularly hardy.
George, by email

Perhaps I didn't make my reason for committing dandelion seed heads to a watery grave clear enough. Dropped in the water there is no danger of volatile seeds of dandelions and their relations ripening, blowing around and infesting other parts of the garden. The seedy debris starts to rot within a week or so (the longer you leave them in the water the better), and then the bucket and contents can be tipped safely on to the compost heap. That goes for all annual weeds: simply dunk the lot, leaves and all, if there is any question of there being ripening seeds amongst them. The delightful bucket-load will start to stink – but you just have to ignore that.

In fact, on reflection, I would not risk weeds in flower in the compost heap (in this I include over-enthusiastic cottage-garden spreaders such as past-their-best forget-me-nots, fennel, verbascum, etc) without first starting to get the rotting process under way, which is what a prolonged dunk does. This is because compost heaps need to generate some pretty high steamy heat right through to destroy seed reliably. In my experience this rarely happens in a normal domestic heap or bin, which has an annoying tendency to stay rather dry at the sides unless stirred almost daily. A further weed-disposal tip: perennial weed roots (ground elder and so on) should always be left to dry in the sun so that they are completely dead before they are added to a compost heap or bin. ❧

THINGS TO CONSIDER IN MAY

❧ Provide individual canes to support vulnerable lily stems, shoots of delphiniums and other perennials with top-heavy flower heads as they grow, in all but the most sheltered gardens. And do it now.

❧ Sapling alert: ash, sycamore and oak seedlings put down tough roots quickly. Winkle them out while they are tiny.

❧ Troughs and containers of summer flowers can be potted up now, but in colder counties may still need to be sheltered from the wind and carefully hardened off.

❧ Blanket weed should be hauled out of ponds: twine it round a cane. Then dose the water with extract of barley straw or put in bags of barley straw. Even a bunch of watercress, hurled into the pond (minus its rubber band), will start to grow, using nutrients that would otherwise support algal growth.

Pruning and snipping
❧ Avoid overcrowding in your beds and borders. Existing plants have still got a long way to grow, so don't be tempted to pack things in.

❧ Early spring-flowering shrubs need to be pruned now, as they fade.

❧ Pulmonarias should have old flower stems removed completely to make way for their new decorative leaves.

❧ Nip off and bin any swollen and mis-shapen buds of day lilies. They contain the larvae of the destructive hemerocallis gall midge.

Summer

June

ON POTTY POSIES AND FLOWER REARRANGING

Faced with the prospect of the sheer bliss of warm summer mornings, my thoughts turned to picking flowers – or rather, *not* picking flowers. Why is it that some gardeners cannot wait to go out of a morning – one pictures the flowing skirt, the slightly battered hat, the slippers and snippers, the family-heirloom Sussex trug – to pick armfuls of long-stemmed loveliness for the house? Delphiniums? Off with their heads! And arms and legs into the bargain, if you want a decent, generous display in the dining room. Ah paeonies! Perfect en masse on the hall table! And wouldn't those lofty white foxgloves look just gorgeous in the inglenook with a branch or two from the variegated pittosporum and some Solomon's seal? Snippety snip.

Meanwhile, others of us flop out there at dawn in our jimjams just to blink at the gloriousness of the splendid, dew-spangled tableau that is our pride and joy, that has taken us months to mastermind, weeks to weed, hours to prop up and now here it all is for a few short weeks of the English summer – untouchable, fabulous. We deadhead daily with reverence, savouring each and every precious sunny morning. We marvel at the way the light changes the whole thing from dawn to dusk, gleaming through peerless translucent beetroot-red foliage or slanting before sunset through the massed floral swathes that are abuzz with hovering insects. Cut any of it for the house? Over our dead bodies!

The most we can bring ourselves to do is pick potty little posies of 'cottage garden' this-and-that (always from stems that 'don't show'), stuffing them into small vases on the kitchen table as a reminder of what we are missing when we get trapped indoors on rainy days, or to give to a very favoured few – hospitalised friends, dinner hosts or much appreciated but sadly housebound elderly neighbours.

All gardeners have their little quirks and foibles, I suppose. I have a friend (who loves flower arranging and is on her church flower rota) whose husband throws a serious marriage-threatening wobbly if she as much as picks a daisy off the lawn (I exaggerate, but only slightly); another who is worse than me and can only bring herself to pick miniature posies to grace tiny antique mustard pots (and invariably wins prizes for them at her local flower show).

And me? I grow my roses specifically for picking on a soulless allotment and the closest I get to raiding my garden proper (apart from picking the aforementioned potty posies, that is) is when I stock my Calamity Can. Anything that is snapped off by the wind, flattened by heavy rain or feline shenanigans, anything too tall, or bending the wrong way and thus spoiling the perfection of the gorgeous visual feast out there, is carefully rescued or culled and stuck in an ancient watering can that stands outside my back door, making the place look like something from the pages of one of those country-lifestyle-fantasy magazines. The Calamity Can's population gets smartened up almost daily in high summer as newcomers are added and oldies falter and fade, and the water is refreshed if it starts to get a bit whiffy. I suppose you could call it flower rearranging.

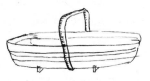

BOX SUCKER

Today I noticed some sort of fluffy white stuff on our small box hedge. At first I thought someone had been shaking out a duster over it but, closer to, I could see it was some kind of blight and is sticky to the touch. Is this likely to be a serious problem?
Hilary, by email

The sticky, fluffy white stuff would indicate that your hedge has an infestation of insects called box suckers (*Psylla buxi*). The damage will not harm the hedge in the long term, nor will the insects migrate to other plants in the garden.

Box sucker is rarely troublesome on plants or hedges that are clipped annually around now, because the very act of clipping off the outer growth of box completely interrupts the insect's lifecycle: box suckers lay eggs on shoot tips in August that hatch out the following April. Nymphs will then feast on the new fresh growth of the box for the next few weeks. Adult suckers are white and dusty-looking, which is what you are seeing. Unless pruned, by late summer the leaves on infested new growth become inwardly curled – somewhat resembling tiny Brussels sprouts. June/July pruning therefore effectively shears off the whole problem, and it would be really wise to do everything you can to pick up all the dropped clippings. It might be a good idea, once the box starts to grow again in August, to treat the hedge with a systemic insecticide. ❧

GETTING CLEVER WITH CLEMATIS

Two readers have clematis queries – par for the course this month. Peter asks how he can keep control of a young *Clematis montana* that he is anxious to keep out of a couple of shrubs for which it is making a beeline. He knows that it was a bit of a bad choice for the boundary fence, but he planted it to please his wife..., etc, etc. There are two ways to tackle this familiar problem. Either you let this rampant clematis (from group 1, the earliest to flower) grow unchecked to fill its allotted space for as long as is possible, and cut it right down to within a couple of feet of the ground immediately after it has flowered every third year or so, making it start again – it will flower the following year on the replacement growth. Or, each year you can cut off its new shoots (starting almost before the thing comes into flower in May) and keep lopping the replacement shoots it makes at intervals during high summer, only allowing it to eventually make a small amount of new growth that will flower the following year. The clematis becomes quite dense, but with regular 'wing-clipping' it does not travel as far so fast.

Jill asks what she should do to the large-flowered blue/mauve clematis that is flowering now, once it has finished. This sounds as though it might be 'The President' – an early-flowering variety from group 2, many of which may flower again if they are very lightly trimmed in June, immediately after they have finished their first major flush. This is easier said than done in all that brittle confusing growth – which is why most gardeners don't bother. However, if you do manage it, and subsequently give these show-off clematis a dose of tomato food as well, the reward may be a few more flowers in the very late summer. Double-flowered varieties often produce a late flush-ette of single flowers quite unlike the early-season ones, which can lead to considerable confusion, of course.

ANTS IN YOUR PLANTS?

Now I am elderly and need things to be low maintenance, I have established deeply cultivated raised beds. My problem is that there is at least one ants' nest in a bed yet to be sown and another in one I have planted up. Is the problem that the beds are too dry? Could I just try flooding them out with a hose? I could also do with reducing the number of nests in what purports to be lawn. Help, please.
Andrew, by email

There are more ants than people, of course, so you are never going to win this one: all you can do is persuade the ants to move elsewhere. Certainly the relatively dry, warm conditions of raised beds make them an attractive nest site for ants, and while they are a mere irritation on a lawn, they can and will do a certain amount of disruption to seedlings in a seed bed with their constant earthworks.

There is a biological control for ants from Nemasys that can be applied from now until September. Called No Ants, it takes the form of a water-in solution containing nest-destroying nematodes that you mix up in a can and apply to the soil, lawn or anywhere the problem manifests itself. ❦

LIQUID ASSETS?

*Gardening experts seem to give conflicting advice about
using water containing washing-up liquid – both as an
insecticide and also as a water-recycling drench for thirsty
plants. I would appreciate your advice.*
Barbara, by email

I agree, there is masses of conflicting stuff here that seems to
confuse a lot of us. I ran my own thoughts past Guy Barter,
chief horticultural advisor at the RHS, and this is what came
out in the wash.

Using a dilution of washing-up liquid as an insecticide is
technically illegal and a bit of a hit and miss affair anyway.
It does actually work, though, by breaking down the outer
protective coating of sap-sucking pests such as green- and
blackfly. But if you use too strong a dilution (and that
depends on the kind of detergent you use – and how are we
to know…), you could harm the plants you are trying to save.
So if you want to be 'green' about it, it is safer to go out and
buy an insecticide containing 'fatty acids' (posh words for
soap). You have to remember that these insecticides act by
contact only, so if you use them rather than systemic
chemicals, you will need to spray repeatedly.

The issue of using 'grey water' – re-using domestic water –
is pretty clear, too. Kitchen washing-up water is fine, although
you should use your common sense and not put any really
greasy stuff on the garden. Water from the washing machine
is fine, too, although dishwasher water is not (because of the
salt). Bath and shower water are also safe to use and can be
relatively easily diverted from the drainage system and used
in moderation to supplement watering with rain water, etc.
However, grey water gets smelly if stored for more than a few
days, and if used exclusively over a very long period with no
rain, it could in theory eventually pollute the soil. My own

view is that it is all a bit of a palaver, but if it really was a matter of life or death (of plants, that is), I would make myself use whatever safe grey water I could get hold of. ❧

AN AILING DWARF LILAC

*Having admired a very healthy dwarf lilac (*Syringa
pubescens *subsp.* microphylla 'Superba') *in a friend's
garden, in the spring I acquired a small plant and put it
in my fairly sunny mixed border. It looked a bit thin but
it had some good flower buds on it. However, just as the
flowers started to open, many of its leaves went grey-ish at
the tips and subsequently fell off. Was this just because
I planted it a bit late, and gave it a shock? Or is there
something a bit more sinister going on?*
Carolyn, by email

It is not the best idea to plant things when they are just about to flower, but in this case it sounds to me as though your little lilac has a (possibly recurring) fungal disease, a mildew of some sort, that it was very probably already harbouring before you bought it. I suspect that if you look carefully at the stems you will see small new buds ready to burst forth with a fresh crop of leaves. This kind of stop/start growth inevitably makes a bush become somewhat thin and threadbare.

I would certainly not give up on this plant. First deadhead it and trim the branches back by a few inches to encourage new shoots that will help thicken up its new growth. Tidy up the soil around the base of the plant (picking up and disposing of any fallen leaves) and apply a fresh organic mulch around it. Then spray the new leaves when they appear with a systemic fungicide such as Systhane Fungus Fighter or FungusClear Ultra by Scotts that will not only kill fungal spores inevitably lingering around but will also prevent the plant from succumbing again. Hopefully you will find that your lilac will remain 'clean' in the future, although a preventative spray as it comes into leaf each year might be a good idea.

This delicate little lilac is, incidentally, an absolute gem and perfect for small gardens, producing delicate pink, scented flowers spasmodically through the summer and into autumn. ❦

YEW BE WARY

My Irish yew, Taxus baccata 'Fastigiata', has suffered badly in strong winds and lost its columnar shape. It has been in the ground for a long time and, up until now, has withstood all weather conditions and always maintained its narrow column shape. What can I do to return it to its former glory?
Dawn, by email

When young and sylph-like, in our climate fastigiate yews make a good substitute for rather more bendy and capricious Mediterranean cypresses. As these upright yews age, their vertical growth widens and at some point – the point yours has clearly reached – the trouble can start, with gales and heavy snow weighing down the branches and generally playing havoc with their overall shape.

You can deal with it two ways, by tying or pruning – or possibly a combination of both. You could tie the branches back into position, or even wire them spirally (in the way that cypresses sometimes are bound up to maintain their shape). Or you could prune back into the branches to just below a point where the splaying starts. New growth will still be in a general upwards direction and will soon hide all the evidence.

I say 'you', but I strongly recommend you get in a reputable tree specialist to do the job. You need someone who really knows what they are doing and who has the right equipment. The Arboricultural Association will provide you with a list of professional tree surgeons in your area. ❦

CHICKENS v. PLANTS

Jane asks if I can recommend plants for large troughs that are 'practically chicken proof'. As I recall, most of the damage done to plants by chickens is done less by their destructive pecking and more by their endless soft-shoe shuffling in search of food in the soil. I would suggest that Jane has to protect her troughs in some way: they would be unlikely to hop up into them if there were some barrier – coarse netting, or some such – through or behind which plants could grow but which would protect their roots and the soil around them.

I have friends who allow their hens out of their run and into their (fenced) vegetable garden 'under supervision' (whatever that means – but I suspect it involves a serious amount of amusement and sedentary gardening-time-wasting). They let this limited free-ranging happen only at certain times of year to let the hens scavenge for grubs, slugs and snails (whose eggs they savour as caviar), presumably at times when there are no precious seedlings to dislodge.

SPANISH STEPS

In the autumn a friend kindly gave me a few seedlings of a lovely little daisy that has invaded steps and paving so easily in her garden. Unfortunately my seedlings have not survived. What is the name of the daisy? Would I do better if I grew it from seed?
Mary, by email

This little daisy that fades from white to pink as it ages seems to be de rigueur, as you say, on well-established steps and terraces in more relaxed gardens, and does much to soften the 'my goodness, that patio has landed from Mars!' look in new ones. It is called *Erigeron karvinskianus*, or you may come across the cultivar 'Profusion', or simply see it labelled as Spanish daisy.

Uprooted seedlings can be quite temperamental, especially those transplanted in the autumn that don't get a chance to become established before the cold weather arrives. You could beg some more seedlings from your friend now and you might find they will do rather better. I have found, however, that the best way to get this daisy to spread around seems to be to encourage nature to take its course. I put mine initially in pots, which I then move around the garden during their first summer. The plants drop an enormous amount of seed that blows around the place, and within a year or two you may actually find yourself tut-tutting over it as you weed it out of various places you would rather it didn't grow. If you have to resort to buying packets of seed – or beg some from a friend – imitate nature and sow them in summer, mixing the seed with a little fine, sandy soil, and brushing it in the gaps in loose-laid paving, steps, etc.

Once established, these daisies will flower constantly from around May, and a generous cut back in August will encourage them to go on right through the autumn. Cold winters will knock them back considerably, but all you have to do in spring is tidy up and cut back any weather-beaten stems on the survivors, and they will start up again. ✤

PHOTINIA WITH SPOTTY LEAVES

I have two plants of Photinia × fraseri *'Red Robin' growing in large tubs (and pruned annually to keep them relatively compact). They did well for years until this time last year they suddenly developed spots on many of their leaves, which then dropped off. This year they have done it again –*

although my neighbour's plants are fine. What is causing the problem and how can I stop it happening again?
Janet, Wanstead, London

It is probably of no comfort to you whatsoever to know that you are just one of many, many gardeners to have experienced this problem in the past year or three. The problem is caused by a fungal leaf spot that seems to affect photinias particularly badly. It is hard to eliminate it completely but you may be able to control it to a tolerable degree. I should add that the older leaves of photinias – and other evergreens for that matter – go into a bit of a decline and drop just as they start to make new ones. It makes perfect plant-sense if you think about it – off-loading the old in favour of the new.

Fungal diseases tend to take hold on plants that are under stress for other reasons. Your containerised photinias need to be given some special treatment – to have the top few inches of soil in their tubs replaced with a fresh mixture of soil-based compost mixed with a little multi-purpose compost, to which a fistful of general fertiliser has been added. The tops of the tubs could then be covered with a mulch of pebbles to retain moisture, and you must make sure that they receive a regular supply of water in the height of the summer. I seem to write this with almost tedious regularity, but this treatment really does go a long way to sorting out many a tubbed shrub problem.

Try to minimise the annual leaf spot attack by picking up and disposing of as many of the fallen leaves as you can. Spraying the whole shrub with a systemic fungicide will help, too. Systhane Fungus Fighter or FungusClear Ultra by Scotts are the ones to go for. 🌿

CLIMBERS IN POTS

I have two summer-flowering jasmines, both in good-sized pots, both having plenty of leaf, but neither seems to want to flower. Can you advise, please?
John, by email

Growing climbers in pots – even 'good-sized pots' – can be tricky. I was told early on in my gardening days that a climber needs to make as much root growth as you expect it to make top growth, and I think this is a helpful picture to keep in your mind. It is therefore not that hard to grow some of the smaller clematis or annual climbers – morning glory, black-eyed Susan, etc – in containers. But those climbers with woody stems, plants of more robust proportions such as wisteria and group 1 clematis (*C. montana, C. armandii* and co) and your summer jasmine, are bound to struggle in the long term, and are far happier and more successful if grown in the ground, where they can make as big a root system as they need to support their growth and flower well. And even given optimum growing conditions, jasmine is a climber that may take four or five years to really get into its stride.

If planting in the ground is not an option, your containers should be as big as you have room for – wooden half-barrels are good, since they stay cool in summer and are relatively well-insulated in winter (another important point to consider). Feed the jasmines each spring, but avoid if you can any fertilisers that are high in nitrogen, which will simply encourage leaf growth at the expense of flowers. Rose food or even tomato food (high in potash) would be better. Every year, remove some of the compost from the top of the tubs and replace it with fresh stuff, and cover the top of the barrel with pebbles to conserve moisture. Really large planters can be disguised to an extent by having pots of pretties placed on the pebbles in summer, the watering of which will in turn benefit the roots of the climber beneath. ❦

IRIS NO-SHOW

Six years ago Julia bought a couple of *Iris* 'Sultan's Palace'. They did so well she gave one plant away and since then the other plant has refused to flower. So in desperation she divided the sulky thing last year in an attempt to revive it and there is still not a flower in sight – from either of the two divisions. What is going wrong? My guess is that when 'doing well' she lost sight of what was what, and accidentally gave away the best part – the outer, newer rhizomes – possibly of both her plants, leaving herself with just the unflowering, exhausted and unproductive older sections. Other possibilities? Lack of direct sun on the rhizomes (because of gradually encroaching plant neighbours) is sometimes the cause of failure to flower in irises, which have to be planted with their rhizomes almost horizontal and to the south side of their leaves, so that they will receive a good direct bake from summer sun.

NOT-SO-ENCHANTING NIGHTSHADE

Joy has an area of woodland in her garden that is infested with a gently running shade- and moisture-loving hooligan that goes by the common name of enchanter's nightshade. Having been away for three months, Joy has returned home to find that one of her five compost bins located in the wood has become invaded by this weed, and wonders what she should do about it.

Enchanter's nightshade's Latin name (for those who like a bit of a digression) is *Circaea lutetiana*, and in classical mythology Circe the witch is said to have used the plant to turn the shipmates of Ulysses into pigs. It is not, however, a poisonous weed like its near-namesake, to which it is not related, deadly nightshade. The plant is a bit of a shortie, producing each year slim-stemmed shoots less than a foot tall, topped by short, skinny spires of rather insignificant white flowers. It is not usually regarded as a major garden scourge, and puts on a pretty innocuous show if crowded out by a profusion of taller plants. (I have it in my stuffed, shady garden, and just rip at it when and if I see it.) Given space and the right conditions, enchanter's nightshade does, however, spread by fine, brittle, white running rhizomes. It is less vigorous than ground elder or bindweed but behaves somewhat like those real garden no-no's in so far as broken-off bits of root will quickly become new, spreading plants.

Joy would do well not to use the compost from the invaded bin in the more important bits of her garden unless she riddles (sieves) out every scrap of white root. Thereafter it would be safest to use it as mulch around woodland plants. She could also, if so inclined, remove the cover of the bin (if there is one) and let the weed grow on a little so that it presents a large leaf area and then knobble it with Roundup.

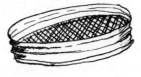

LILY POLLEN ON YOUR CLOTHES?

Maria asked if I know how to get rid of the orange, apparently indelible stain. One's first instinct is to brush off the pollen, which is, I learnt to my cost (and had it confirmed when I went online to seek help, as one does nowadays), an absolute no-no. As is sponging it with a damp cloth (I have done that too, and made things considerably worse). One thing you can and should do immediately is 'blot' off the worst using sticky tape. A powerful pre-laundry stain remover should do the rest.

IRIDESCENT BEETLES ON AROMATIC HERBS

Tricia found two attractive iridescent-striped, ladybird-sized beetles on her lavender last year. This year there are scores of them, and they are now living on her rosemary. She asks if she should be worried. These are rosemary beetles (*Chrysolina americana*) and they also favour lavender, sages and perovskia. The beetles lay eggs on the leaves in late summer and autumn and during mild winter weather. The larvae feed on leaves in early spring and then pupate in the ground around the bushes before emerging as adults. You can either pick the beetles and larvae off (or shake the bushes over newspaper), or spray with an insecticide (Provado Ultimate Bug Killer Ready to Use is suitable for edible herbs) when the plants are not in flower (thus not harming bees). This is a relatively new pest that is spreading northwards.

PRUNING PITTOSPORUM – AND OTHER EVERGREENS

I have a lovely **Pittosporum tenuifolium** *'Silver Queen', which is outgrowing its position. To what extent will it tolerate pruning? I have snipped back small amounts but it really needs something more drastic.*
Barbara, by email

Despite gardeners' understandable reluctance to take it on board, it is perhaps encouraging to know that the vast majority of evergreens (one well-known exception is the infamous × *Cuprocyparis leylandii*) can be cut back quite hard and will fairly quickly shoot out from brown wood. Thus even overgrown rhododendrons, camellias and hedging plants such as yew, box, laurel and privet can be pretty much butchered if necessary and will eventually come back smiling – although it may take a couple of years for those that flower to do so on the new growth they make. *Pittosporum tenuifolium* is another such and indeed it is just as well, since the very elegant 'Silver Queen' and several of its relations grow extremely rapidly.

The best time to prune evergreens is in late spring/early summer, when all danger of frost nipping at subsequent new growth is past and the shrubs are just about to put on a major growth spurt. I feel I should take the opportunity to enlarge on this subject: these pittosporums are not fully hardy north of that imaginary line that goes through Watford. If they suffer patchy frost damage – often on their eastern or northern sides – the affected bare stems must eventually be cut right out as they will not regenerate. Waiting a few weeks and then

70

carrying out some pretty hard pruning may be the only way to recover the shrub's good looks, although if the damage is not too dire of course, the new growth on branches of the rest of the shrub will simply 'close ranks' over the gap. 🌿

WRESTLING WITH AN ENEMY

London *desperada* Myra has a plague of houttuynia – originally 'donated' by a friend 30 years ago (beware, dear readers, of gardeners bearing gifts...). She has tried digging this horrid little spreader out and failed. She has also tried to smother it under membranes and paint it with herbicidal unguents. Now what, she asks?

Myra can dig, fork, riddle and twiddle for all she is worth, but she would do better, I feel, to treat this as a true garden enemy – as if it were ground elder – and knobble it with one of the maximum-strength glyphosate weedkillers such as Roundup Ultra 3000 when it is in full growth, following the instructions on the packaging to the letter. First she has to rescue any of her plants that have been swamped by the houttuynia. These should be dug up and their roots washed so that those of the invading foe can be identified and winkled out. The good plants should then be temporarily grown in pots of loam-based compost until they can be returned to their homes when the coast is clear.

The night before she does the deed she should give the condemned weeds a drink (apparently, generous watering plumps up leaves and makes them more receptive). Any re-growth should be allowed to leaf up and then be similarly clobbered. The aforementioned coast may not be clear until next spring. Horrid, depressing advice. Sorry Myra.

HARVESTING HERBS

Clare would like advice about picking herbs for maximum flavour. Many flowers give off the best scent in the evening; is there a variation in flavour or aroma amongst culinary herbs, she asks? Here's what Jekka McVicar, the herb specialist, has to say, plus tips on how to make chilli and basil oils, since Veronica and others have asked about this, too.

In summer months Jekka simply picks fresh herbs just before she needs them in the kitchen. Gluts of parsley and tarragon can be frozen, of course, and as with all summer herbs, they are at their best when the leaves are dry but before they get baked by afternoon sun.

If you intend to dry herbs (including lavender), it is best to harvest them at the stage of their cycle when they are at their most powerfully aromatic, which is just before they come into flower. Once picked they should then be tied up in small loose bunches and hung up in a cool place. Jekka says that on no account should they be placed near a source of heat or in the sun in order to speed up the process – she simply hangs bunches for drying in her spare room and leaves them for a few weeks.

For basil oil you make a cold infusion. Pick a handful of basil shoots (leaves still attached to their stems) and put them in a glass or china bowl and cover with good olive oil. It is very important to make absolutely sure that the basil is totally immersed in the oil with at least an inch of oil over the top of it. Cover the bowl with clingfilm and leave it for about four weeks before straining it through a coffee filter (to remove odd bits and pieces as well as all the leaves and stems) and bottling it in sterilised bottles. Chilli oil is made in the same way – you cut or crush the chillies before you immerse them. Bottles filled with oil made from your own herbs make great presents for friends – you can recycle interesting ones (I made chilli oil one year in recycled scarlet wine bottles – I can't imagine what was in them originally) or buy smart ones from Lakeland (lakeland.co.uk).

MAGNOLIA GRANDIFLORA

A little reassurance for Andy's friend, whose magnolia (in suitably slightly acid but slightly dry soil) has not produced a flower after 14 years. These trees are notorious for the length of time it takes for them to start flowering. While he is waiting, Andy's friend should not overdose the tree with high-nitrogen fertiliser, but should perhaps try giving it a feed with sulphate of potash during the growing season to try to encourage flower-bud production, and a moisture-retaining mulch of leaf mould or composted bark each spring.

THINGS TO CONSIDER IN JUNE

❋ Shrubs that have flowered since January should now have been pruned, or be about to be pruned. Shred your shrub prunings and add them to your compost bin between layers of grass, etc.

❋ Keep up the deadheading to encourage your herbaceous plants to develop more flower buds rather than going to seed. Remove stems as well (down to a leaf joint or lower flower bud), for aesthetic reasons.

❋ Give late-flowering clematis a kick-start with the application of high-potash tomato food.

❋ Cut back one or two of the best-coloured wallflowers almost to the bone and they will go an extra mile for you next year – they are biennials.

❋ Potted citrus bushes and other conservatory and houseplants will also enjoy a spell outside for a couple of months in a sheltered place.

❋ And finally, don't be too blinkered about your own plot. Visit other people's gardens for inspiration and light relief.

Focus on lawns
❋ Mow lawns little and often on a slightly higher setting, for a tougher and more weed/moss-free lawn in the long term.

❋ If adding grass clippings to compost bins in quantity, stir them into the mixture below 24 hours later, to take advantage of the heat they will have created, and to stop them forming a sludgy mass.

❋ Winkle out plantains with an old kitchen fork and spot-weed dandelions with Roundup Weedkiller Gel.

❋ If you haven't time to mow the lawn, at least neaten the edges with shears – which makes the whole garden look tidier.

July

THE LOWEST OF THE LOW?

Dare I say it, dear readers: I can get just a teeny bit downcast by your endless planting disasters and with having again and again to remind you how to rid yourselves of assorted undesirables. The constant drip, drip of queries from gardeners oh-so-badly wanting to get things right, but whose sieve-like memories have necessitated the compilation of not one, but two volumes of *Thorny Problems* to adorn the loo bookshelf, can present a real challenge. Then, a couple of times a year perhaps, out of the blue comes a complete non-gardener (how he/she ever discovered the Thorny Problems page beats me) asking how best to go about taming/ planting their outdoor space (generally part of a new and possibly a first property, thus blank canvasses all round), so as to make it the *absolutely lowest* of low-maintenance gardens EVER. All he or she clearly wants to do is improve the view of the shabby outdoors from the chic indoors, so that the garden will not detract from the value of the property, and to thereafter maintain sufficient control of it to avoid neighbourly disputes. Offering useful advice to the determinedly un-horticultural presents, not surprisingly, a challenge of a different kind.

Like most gardeners, I have pretty clear ideas as to what to me makes a satisfying garden, and it is not really fair, I think, for me to impose these on uninterested innocents and lead them, as it were, up a complicated garden path – halfway along which they are bound to get lost. And actually it is extremely hard to be genuinely helpful on even the simplest level without knowing some basics about the general aspect. Are we talking about a bleak rectangle of builders' rubble infested with weeds? Or a patch dominated by a blank brick wall/indiscreet neighbour's badly screened bathroom window? It is, of course, unlikely to be a case of dressing up far-reaching views of the Yorkshire Moors, or creating a 'foredrop' to an acre of gorgeous woodland, now is it?

Ultimately, whatever other low-maintenance features may be needed to create a garden of sorts (flowering evergreens should get a mention here), and banishing totally any ideas of planting a row of conifers, totally obliterating everything with paving or that dreadful alternative, decking – I find myself homing in on the simplest ingredients that together can make something green, peaceful and pleasing out of a seemingly unlovable patch of ground.

Grass is actually low maintenance, and even determined anti-gardeners can find a certain pleasure in sitting on a mower (i.e. go into the prairie-harvesting fantasy) or walking behind one (this can involve the six-pack/waistline enhancement fantasy). I would therefore suggest that the area in question be initially weedkilled with glyphosate (to get rid of docks, thistles and other vigorous 'unwanteds' and create a clean-ish slate), after which the infertile-looking soil can be sown with a suitable grass and summer wildflower mix. The flowers will actually benefit from the lack of richness in the soil, holding their own against the grasses – and both will grow up and look tolerably pretty for weeks on end in high summer, then can be mown lawn-short from August to November and again during March and April the next spring.

The other low-maintenance idea involves deciduous trees: a small group strategically placed and planted quite close together (yes, yes, inevitably elegant white-trunked silver birches spring to mind because I love them so much), makes a good focal point and will delicately screen any 'unsightlies'. Add to this a pretty seat and a summer-mown, neat, slightly curving path leading to it through the grass and flowers from the back door and voila: a tranquil 'garden' of sorts.

COTTAGE GARDENER, BEWARE

Enthusiastic emailer Beth has just moved to a cottage in Herefordshire. She has worked out from things I have written that my own garden style is 'relaxed' and wants me to list my favourite cottage-garden self-seeders. The following list comes with a big caveat: the self-seeding cottage garden is not necessarily an easy option, particularly for beginners. It needs hawk-eyed maintenance, or it becomes a jungle where one or two plants dominate. But here goes: aquilegia, Welsh poppy – yellow and orange (*Meconopsis cambrica*), various subtly coloured forms of field poppy (*Papaver rhoeas*) and opium poppy (*P. somniferum*), sweet rocket (*Hesperis matronalis*), *Lamium orvala* – a little-known raspberry-red-flowered tall dead nettle, *Smyrnium perfoliatum* – a bright lime-headed biennial cow parsley relation, and sweet cicely (*Myrrhis odorata*) –

another c p relation, *Geranium pyrenaicum* 'Bill Wallis', perennial stock, *Verbascum chaixii* 'Album', honesty (*Lunaria annua*), bronze fennel, knautia, *Tellima grandiflora* Rubra Group, Miss Willmott's ghost (*Eryngium giganteum* or the similar cultivar *E.g.* 'Silver Ghost'), *Astrantia major* and foxgloves. I could go on and on...

However, instead I will squeeze in here a useful tip: that The Cottage Garden Society (thecottagegardensociety.org.uk) produces a booklet called *A Cottage Garden Planner* – a helpful guide to the subject by Pat Collison and Margaret Mason.

SHADING A CONSERVATORY

I have spent too long scouring my desk and trawling emails looking for a mislaid letter: Mrs Nameless from Somewhere needs advice on what to plant in her conservatory for some summer shade. Her neighbour has a rather rampant grapevine, which she regards as too untidy. (I do so agree – all those crumply leaves that drop in the Pimm's...)

Logically, if shade is only needed in the summer months, then the plant to grow will be one that can be cut down in the winter but is vigorous enough to leg it up to the roof by June, needing only relatively lightweight support and minimal care when it gets there. Icing on the cake would be provided by non-stop flowering until the autumn. This is quite a tall order, as few 'easy' plants will fit the whole bill.

In my view there is one such plant that would do it all for Mrs

Nameless and that is *Ipomoea indica*, a tender, vigorous (indeed, rampant if not cut back in late winter), perennial relation of our much-loved annual morning glory that carries large leaves and a summer-long succession of deeper, bluer flowers that fade to magenta on their second day. It needs plenty of root room to support all the annual growth, it is true, but when in full sail it is the most magnificent sight. I saw it growing wild in Nepal and found that a local nursery in East Sussex (perryhillnurseries.co.uk) sells young rooted plants each spring.

Along with an apology to Mrs Nameless for the administrative lapse, I will take the opportunity to thank Jill from Whitchurch who has been growing *Ipomoea indica* (or a close relation thereof) in her conservatory for the past 15 years without knowing its precise name and sent me a watercolour she had painted of its flowers, together with a request for identification. Receiving it quite made my day.

HEATWAVE TACTICS

After weeks of sudden, glorious and intense summer sunshine, I produced some advice about how to stop gardens from dropping dead in the heat. Take heed, dear readers, such extraordinary weather may happen again... and the following list of priorities may be helpful.

Plants in containers are most vulnerable, especially small ones containing annuals. Group them together in the shade. Concentrate on applying water slowly to the big immovable and important things – the tubs of camellias, hydrangeas, acers and other woodlanders that hate hot roots. If the butt water they prefer is running short, tap water won't harm them in the short or medium term.

Newly planted trees, shrubs and perennials will appreciate a slow drench (at least half a big watering can each) once every few days, to encourage them to make deep roots.

So resist the temptation to give them less more often. Scrape away mulches before you water and replace them afterwards.

Even established plants may wilt at mid-day in extreme heat, but are unlikely to die. Make a note to mulch more next spring.

Droughted lawns always green up again – don't water them.

Finally: water slowly and thoroughly in the cool of the evening so that everything stays moist for as long as possible. Aim your watering can or hose at the soil around each plant, rather than at leaves, and water deeply an area about the size of each plant's 'canopy'.

GOLDEN GRASS – FRIEND OR FOE?

I casually admired what you might call a 'drift' of yellow-leaved grass in a friend of a friend's garden and she quickly bent down and wrenched out a small clump of it and gave it to me to take home. Have I unwittingly invited in one of your so-called hooligans to my garden?
Miranda, by email

I suspect your lovely newcomer is *Milium effusum* 'Aureum', also known as Bowles's golden grass, which is a useful short-lived perennial that seeds around just enough but not too much. Bright little self-seedlings are easy to spot and winkle out, and those that you allow to survive and prosper will form the basis of a small colony (lovely with forget-me-nots and wallflowers) that will ebb and flow and pop up here and there indefinitely, particularly useful in light or dappled shade where the soil is not too dry. You can always 'adjust the flow' by moving individual plants around in spring. Clumps cut back after they have flowered will re-shoot and form a neat golden tuft for late summer and early autumn before dying away for the winter.

So, to answer your question: this one is very much a goodie, I think. ❦

LIVERWORT BETWEEN PAVING STONES

I have a problem with liverwort growing between the paving slabs on my patio. If allowed it would stray on to my lawn. Glyphosate seems to have little effect on it. Using

*a flame gun was only temporarily successful and I even
tried scraping out the paving crevices, but the liverwort still
comes back. How can I see this menace off permanently?*
David, by email

Poor drainage and lack of soil cultivation are largely to blame
for the proliferation of this hard-to-control primitive, ground-
hugging, algae- and moss-related weed of damp and shady
places. Glyphosate, it is acknowledged, is only really effective
in this case if a wetting agent such as washing-up liquid is
added to it, which helps to prevent it simply running off the
slightly shiny, scale-like 'leaves', and of course can only be
used where the liverwort is growing away from wanted plants.

Reader Gillian sent me a helpful tip she had learned from
a local nurserywoman who, as an experiment, sprinkled
sulphate of iron on to liverwort growing on the surface of
potted plants. Sulphate of iron on its own (it is the moss-
killing 'ingredient' in lawn-care products) should, as Gillian
points out, not be used willy-nilly since it is fairly strong stuff,
but it should be safe to use, wearing gloves of course, and
should do the trick if applied carefully between the cracks
of your paving stones. 🌿

ROSE ON A NORTH WALL

*Having read an article recommending 'Madame Alfred
Carrière' for north-facing walls, we planted one a few years
ago. We take off the previous year's growth in the winter
and feed in the spring. We get lots of new stems but very
few flowers. What are we doing wrong?*
James, by email

'Madame Alfred' is indeed often recommended as a rose that
will do well on a north-facing wall, as is the almost thornless
'Zéphirine Drouhin'. However, and it is a big however, there

are north walls and there are North Walls. By which I mean that some north-facing walls have a basically open aspect and receive more light than others – either because they are lower, or are not surrounded by other shade-giving trees or buildings, or are even simply painted white. All roses need at least four hours of summer sunshine in order to do well (this is a David Austin dictum, not just a Yemm one), and your wall may be simply too dark.

Another factor may be your pruning regime. 'Taking off the previous year's growth' may not be doing the rose many favours. Climbing roses flower best on young-ish growth that is trained more or less horizontally, and while climbers need to have the short shoots that flowered the previous season pruned back in winter to within about two buds from where they join the structural (horizontal) branches, any new strong, potential structural branches that come from the base of the rose should be left un-pruned and simply trained in as they grow to replace, in due course, some of the older ones. You may be over-pruning, in which case your rose has to put an awful lot of energy into just growing back each year. ❧

LIFE ON THE VERGE

Excited by the magnificence of the ox-eye daisies on un-mown grass verges near to where I live in an East Sussex village, I expressed the opinion that it would be rather good if more garden owners were to loosen their stays a little and stop trying to make little slips of grass outside their houses resemble extensions of their very smart, weekly mown lawns. I was surprised at the response: not one neat-and-tidy lawn freak wrote to defend themselves or justify their activities – maybe they decided that there was no point since I appeared to have completely lost the plot.

While an extraordinary number of readers agreed with me wholeheartedly.

As a reminder: ox-eye daisies are as tough as they are (in my view) charming, often regarded as invasive weeds, but easily controlled by deadheading. They can withstand close mowing after flowering in late summer and again in early spring, and will come back and flower year after year, creating flower drifts carried well above the height of the otherwise un-manicured grass in which they grow. Their seeds germinate easily in autumn or spring and to an agreeable extent will even compete with rapidly sprouting grass (which less plucky wildflowers cannot). Maintenance of an ox-eye daisy and grass verge requires mowing (collecting the clippings) only twice a year, with a possible extra late autumn mow to neaten it up for the winter.

I am fairly determined, in the absence of any attention from council strimmers, to keep my tiny verge wild but also to make it more attractive. So last spring I gave nature a helping hand – I mowed the grass extremely short, surreptitiously dug out a few coarser grass tussocks and popped in some small ox-eye daisy plantlets ('weeds' found in my garden), which performed beautifully. Then I carried out what I can only describe as 'assisted self-seeding', picking off the ripe seed heads and strewing them around over the verge, but only after I had mowed the whole area, again extremely short. So I've had an even better show this year, and anticipate it improving for years to come.

BACK TO THE FUCHSIA

In recent years my fuchsias have been flowering poorly. In case this was caused by capsid bugs, I have been very diligent before the plants start sprouting, clearing up fallen leaves and bits and pieces. I read an article that warned gardeners of a new pest affecting fuchsias, but it gave no description of what we should look out for. Could you enlighten us? I am hoping this new pest is not the cause of my problem.
Julie, Coventry

Scary articles on new gardening problems – like those about health issues – are with us to stay, it seems. This 'new' fuchsia pest is called the fuchsia gall mite (*Aculops fuchsiae*) and has been with us on mainland UK for several years; it was first noticed in the Channel Islands, from where it is presumed to have spread on affected plants to some southern counties. The microscopic mite is a sap-sucker, feasting on shoot tips, at the same time secreting substances that distort and damage the developing buds. As an infestation takes hold, brown-ish, yellow-ish, badly distorted growth appears where you would expect pristine young leaves and flower buds to be. This damage is quite different from the puckered and black-dotted ragged shoot tips that result from a capsid bug attack. These gall mites are specific to fuchsias – the various types of capsid bug are not.

There is no chemical available to gardeners that will reliably defend against or control this pest, but it could still just about be nipped in the bud if affected plants have all damaged shoots cut off as soon as infestation is suspected or, better still, if the entire plants are destroyed. While they can produce several generations in a single growing season, these gall mites do not survive frost, so as they do spread seriously northwards, they are likely to become a real problem in very sheltered, city gardens and on tender glasshouse-grown plants. ❦

PLANTING CLEMATIS IN SUMMER

I have a feeling you are going to tell me I was unwise to buy a Clematis *'Madame Julia Correvon' in full flower to climb over a shrub in my new garden, but I couldn't resist it and I am now dying to plant it. Should I or shouldn't I?*
Clare, by email

It all depends on the weather. In a wet year, it is probably safe for all of us to plant new high summer 'impulse' purchases, because the soil is unusually damp. Though bear in mind that the ground may be damp in places where it is usually bone dry for much of the time (under or around big trees, for example), so you have to use your noddle a bit when deciding on a planting site. But if you must plant now, come rain or shine, there are steps you can take to maximise success.

Prepare a planting hole that is at least half as deep again as the height of the black pot and at least twice as wide. Mix the removed soil 50/50 with good compost and a fistful of bonemeal or some slow-release fertiliser. Loosen the soil at the bottom of the hole, incorporate some more compost and sprinkle some Rootgrow around.

Place the de-potted clematis in the hole, making sure that its roots come into contact with the Rootgrow. Start to backfill with the soil/compost mixture and, halfway through the operation, water the plant into place. Finish the job and firm the area gently with your foot. Your clematis should, if you have done the job well, have the bottom couple of inches of its slim and vulnerable stems below the level of the soil. No further watering should be necessary at this point.

Mulch around the plant with more compost, and as a precaution, apply a barrier to deter snails (e.g. a wide swathe of Slug Gone, or a few slug pellets around the plant).

Leave the supporting bamboo canes and green ties in situ until the clematis has started climbing into the host shrub.

And for anyone contemplating moving a clematis, see October, page 142. ❧

A SOLAR HA HA?

A bit of not-very-horticultural silliness that made me chuckle... I went to a posh girls' lunch recently (a rare occurrence, dear readers; normally lunch for me is BBC – that's bloody-bread-and-cheese, in case you were wondering – munched inelegantly on the hoof). In due course, gardening matters cropped up as they tend to do, and Catherine, sitting next to me, announced cheerfully that she had solved all by herself the appalling problem of getting plants to work in the thin, arid soil on a long steep and sunny south-facing bank. Even though the area is out of sight of the house, her lack of success peeved her. So she simply 'planted' a long row of solar panels. Now instead of weeding and watering, she happily counts the kilowatts. Is this the way forward?

TIME TO GO?

I have three phormiums in my two gardens (one is a holiday home in Dorset). All are very large and have suffered badly in the wind and rain. In the past I have removed old and ugly leaves with secateurs, but this year I feel drastic action is needed. Should I raze them to the ground with a hedge trimmer? Will they grow back and look smart again? Digging out is not an option.
Susan, Sunningdale (and Dorset)

Regular readers will know exactly what I am going to suggest. I, along with countless other gardeners, was once seduced by this thuggish alien that for a few years and mild winters provided an interesting 'new look'. Their colourful vertical sword-like leaves and (in due course) exotic-looking flowers on stiff lofty stems became an almost obligatory 1990s garden feature. I have since come to loathe them: so many of them have gradually become the most hideous overbearing blight – massive in old age and battered by a couple of winters – in so many otherwise comfortably mature gardens.

So Susan, even if you did rather savagely hedge-trim your plants to resuscitate them, I doubt they would ever regain their good looks. Yet I urge you to go ahead and do it. Once

they are reduced to ruins, you will see that they actually consist of several fan-shaped sections. Believe me, it will probably only take a few vigorous sessions with a sharp spade to get them out – lock, stock and barrel – even though you say that digging them out is not an option. Bag up all the bits and bin them (they won't compost well), and live with the resulting big gaps for the rest of the summer while you think of something with which to replace them. I bet you sigh with relief once they are gone, and that both of your gardens will look all the better for their absence. So just do it. ❦

ANY OTHERS FOR THE CHOP?

I am delighted by the effect of Chelsea chopping my sedum 'Autumn Joy'. Which other plants would benefit from this?
Patricia, by email

The so-called 'Chelsea chop' (cutting back perennials in late May – see page 42) is referred to a lot one way or another, and you are not the first reader to ask this question.

First, it should be said, there are some perennials that you would *not* chop – the most obvious of which are spire-formers grown for their vertical presence in the garden. A dumpy verbascum or chubby hollyhock with several stems just doesn't quite live up to the dream, does it? And you really wouldn't want to chop at a clump of herbaceous geraniums, either, or alstroemeria, for example, which don't produce side shoots that would snap into action and multiply their flower power. In my experience the perennials that respond the best are the various daisies. *Anthemis tinctoria* gets very lofty and floppy in rich soil and is therefore hard to support, as are old-fashioned shasta daisies and heleniums. My phlox also respond really well, and I have a suspicion that *Campanula lactiflora* might do so, too. I tried Chelsea chopping a rather lax shrubby perovskia, and was pleasantly surprised.

86

Details about how you actually execute the Chelsea chop, either by shearing the whole plant or just chopping every other stem, is described in a great book by Tracy DiSabato-Aust, *The Well-Tended Perennial Garden* (Timber Press). ❧

LATE SUMMER MILDEW

I'm sorry if this is a very obvious question, but why do my phlox have mildew and what should I do about them?
Elaine, Ferndown, Dorset

I get lots of questions about mildew – both kinds. In the first half of the season, all the angst tends to be about downy mildew (botrytis), a white furry mould that can prevail where the air is constantly damp and leaves and stems are moist. This is the kind of mildew that can kill off a tray of seedlings overnight and rots the stems of soft-wood cuttings. It should not be confused with the various forms of late summer mildew, which show as dusty white deposits on leaves and stems. This one can be prevalent in congested borders and on plants grown against hot walls where soil becomes dry, and spoils the growth of all sorts of garden plants.

Some plants – roses and sweet peas, for example – are notoriously plagued by mildew, and some aren't. Amongst perennials, phlox frequently fall victim (as do monardas, incidentally). There are, however, some varieties that are known to be less susceptible than others: *Phlox paniculata* 'David' (white) and 'Starfire' (vivid red) both do well and are totally mildew free.

The answer to the second part of your question can be summed up as follows: liberal mulching with organic matter in late spring in order to conserve moisture in the soil around your phlox roots, followed by preventative spraying with a systemic fungicide (such as Systhane Fungus Fighter or FungusClear Ultra by Scotts), as they grow and fill out in June. ❧

THINGS TO CONSIDER IN JULY

Borders and flowers
❊ Keep eyes peeled for wisps of willowherb and various slender dandelion relations that have nuisance windborne seeds.

❊ Cut away stems and tired-looking foliage of plants that have flowered, such as *Alchemilla mollis* (lady's mantle) and nepeta (catmint) and they will leaf up quickly and may even flower again.

❊ Perennial violas (e.g. *V. cornuta*) can be cut right back and given a liquid feed. They will flower again within a week or three.

❊ Feed annuals and flowering plants in containers every two weeks with a high-potash liquid feed (tomato food is good).

❊ Watch out for snail activity (usually nocturnal) on the young foliage of dahlias and bedding plants.

❊ Feed roses with proprietary rose food to encourage continued healthy growth and optimum performance of repeat flowerers after their first flush. Apply the granules in a circle around the base, avoiding contact with the stems.

To seed or not to seed?
❊ Save newly ripened seeds of hardy annuals such as 'Fairy Wings' poppies and nigella to sow in early autumn or spring.

❊ Conversely, the seeds of related umbels *Smyrnium perfoliatum* and *Myrrhis odorata* (sweet cicely) are best sown really fresh.

❊ The first flowers of spire-forming perennials (e.g. delphiniums and foxgloves) can be stopped from going to seed if you cut them down to just above small secondary spires (which will flower better as a result).

Secateurs at the ready

❉ Very gently and carefully trim back the growth of clematis that finished flowering this month (group 2). No more than a couple of feet (60cm) of spent flower shoots here and there.

❉ Prune laurel hedges with care, using secateurs or loppers to remove stems/branches rather than shears or a hedge trimmer (the resulting chopped leaf edges look ugly). Laurel leaves rot extremely poorly, and release cyanide if you shred them en masse to speed up the process. They are thus better consigned to the council green-waste system.

❉ Be ruthless about foliage that hides paths or impedes access: better cut out/off than trodden on or bashed.

❉ *And finally...* Fight the downside of hot-weather sloth. Don't idly throw anything (plant ties, old labels, champagne corks) into the back of your borders that you don't want to have to pick up in November.

'CAVEAT EMPTOR' SALE

August

'BARGAIN' PLANTS

We've all done it at one time or another. The rot starts when you see a glorious something-or-other – usually a shrub, a climber, or at worst a rose – in full sail in someone else's garden. The hankering process starts instantly with daydreams about where it will fit perfectly in your own garden – as a replacement, perhaps, for something ancient and ugly the previous owners planted and that you have always hated. Sanity slips quietly out of the back gate as the daydreams rapidly become a full-blown nightmare when you decide that you can bear the *Ancientia formerownerensis uglissimus* not a single minute longer and that it just *has* to be dug up *immediately* (very possibly on the hottest day of the year). Faced with a gaping hole in the garden tableau bang in the middle of summer, the goose-chase immediately begins for your shrubby/climbing inamorata: the *RHS Plant Finder* is consulted, phone calls are made, many, many blanks are drawn. In desperation you start rooting about amongst the has-beens at random roadside nurseries, ignoring the little voice in your head that tells you this is the very worst time of year for a full-on shrub-hunt, when the nurseries are having a quick zizz recovering from bedding-plant fever and before October – 'the start of the gardening year' – when they re-stock. But suddenly, lo! There it is, 50 per cent off in the Bargain Corner with all the other kicked-about bits and pieces. And you buy it, thrilled, and take it home and plant it in August, and even possibly go away on holiday the next day – and it almost always fails. Maybe not immediately, but it fails.

So, some advice for all you out there with a pitiful 'bargain plant' sitting outside the back door only scantily clad in leaves, possibly even with roots sticking out of the bottom of its pot – looking about as comfortable as someone who's been dancing all night at a party in tight shoes. My advice to you is DON'T PLANT IT. By all means now you've got it, do your best for it: ease it out of its container and pot it on into one a size or two larger, using loam-based compost. Trim off its crispy bits, cutting back to where hopefully some new growth is showing, water it, stand it in the shade and don't let it dry out. If it perks up well by October, plant it then. If it still looks wretched, it means the roots were too badly damaged to recover and may never do so. Go back to square one, do some sensible research and buy yourself a decent replacement. (Oooh, she's bossy, that Helen Yemm.)

COW PARSLEY LOOKALIKES

I'm a big fan of white-flowered umbels, which seems now to be the smart way to refer to members of the plant family *Umbelliferae* (or *Apiaceae*), a.k.a. the cow parsley family. I love *Ammi majus* and another close relation *Orlaya grandiflora*, but they are not the easiest annuals to grow (certainly the latter only really makes a good summer plant if seed is germinated under glass the previous autumn). I adore sweet cicely (*Myrrhis odorata*) too and have even been known to let cow parsley seed around to a degree. Both of these look classy growing informally in dappled shade amongst stripy hostas such as 'Frances Williams' (*sieboldiana*) and the best white astrantias (*A. major* subsp. *involucrata* 'Shaggy'). And now I grow another perennial from the same family, *Cenolophium denudatum*. It flowers later and for longer than the other two and has slightly more robust and shiny foliage. I find it combines well with all sorts. It looks elegant around white phlox and I thoroughly recommend that anyone with the space for a spread of macleaya plonks some plants of cenolophium in amongst it to provide a dramatic contrast.

RENOVATING STUMPY HEUCHERA

I advised Sue on the maintenance of her colourful heucheras when she complained that her plants had become very leggy by the end of their third summer – and much less attractive as a result. I told her that to simply cut off the stumpy shoots and expect the plants to rally was a bit of a hit and miss solution, and that it was better to lift and divide plants in autumn or spring. I also decided, as often happens in the wake of readers' queries actually, to carry out an experiment on a couple of my own plants, cutting off a couple of the shoots as close to ground level as possible (taking stem cuttings, effectively) and simply poking them into the soil and keeping an eye on them in the hopes that they would spontaneously root. To my complete delight they have done so, and have become thriving young plants, producing plenty of bright new leaves. Maybe this is common practice amongst experienced and besotted heucheraphiles, of whom there are now scores, of course, and maybe it is just a case of your columnist being 'last with the news' (not for the first time...). However, I thought it was worth passing the information on. Poking the stumps into pots of sandy compost would be a slightly more sensible and flexible option, of course.

THE POISON SEASON

Emailers Gill and Ken both noticed somewhat strident interlopers in their gardens recently and sent me pictures of them. In both cases they had unwittingly been cultivating the highly poisonous thorn apple (*Datura stramonium*), now sporting large and very distinctive prickly seedpods. Christopher emailed a picture of another slightly dodgy alien that turned up in his garden: American pokeweed (*Phytolacca americana*), an eye-catching thing that carries luscious-looking (but actually poisonous) clusters of wine-red seeds at this time of year. If he doesn't like it and doesn't want it around next year, I suggest he carefully pulls it up before its seeds ripen.

While pokeweed is considered by some to be an imposing addition to the garden, both these plants can be introduced unwittingly into gardens via imported bird seed. This is no reason to stop feeding our birds, I should stress. Most things that turn up in the garden as a result of feeding birds are pretty harmless – millet, the odd rogue sunflower or maybe a few small hemp plants. But it may serve to remind us to be just slightly wary of letting any old stuff grow to maturity and set seed around bird-feeding stations.

TAP WATER

What are you supposed to do when it hasn't rained properly for weeks and all the water butts are empty? Margaret worries about her three potted azaleas; Peter from Hertfordshire about the camellia he has just planted in a tub of ericaceous compost; while Georgia fears for her similarly planted blueberries.

Some plants (such as those above and many others that are referred to sometimes as 'woodlanders') cannot take up nutrients unless they have their roots tucked into soil that has a low pH (and is therefore slightly acid). Lime in tap water can, over time, raise the pH of soil, making it slightly alkaline, and these lime-sensitive plants will eventually show their distress if they have to be watered exclusively from the tap: the colour of their leaves will turn from a good, healthy-looking green to a pale and more insipid shade, often with darker green veins. If uncorrected, growth slows down and plants may eventually simply turn up their toes.

The condition is called lime-induced chlorosis. Watering sensitive plants, particularly those in containers, routinely with rain water – which is, of course, lime free – is the best way to avoid problems of this kind, but watering them less or not at all when rain water is in short supply is merely going to put them under stress of another kind. You can prevent or correct lime-induced chlorosis by giving acid-loving plants a tonic of iron (as in Sequestrene) once a year at the beginning of the growing season. This is a particularly useful trick if plants are growing in garden soil that has only slightly the 'wrong' pH. There is also a liquid feed for acid-lovers: Maxicrop Seaweed plus Sequestered Iron (the one in the blue bottle), which can be added to tap water and given to acid-lovers every few weeks during the growing season.

And the bottom line is? In the short to medium term the use of tap water on acid-loving plants is not going to kill them.

PRUNING A BEECH HEDGE

I have a mature beech hedge that I wish to cut back. When is the best time to do this without damaging future growth?
John, by email

One of the best things about a beech hedge is the fact that, although deciduous, it provides a good screen all year round by retaining its old leaves for the winter, only dropping them when new growth is made in spring. Annual pruning is therefore recommended as a late summer job, so that the hedge has time to leaf up again before the autumn. In my experience, those who cut beech hedges in August or thereabouts do so rather timidly (reluctant to remove all the leaf growth, particularly from the sides). Thus over time beech hedges tend to become really 'fat', and eventually need more radical treatment.

If your hedge has not been cut back for some time and has become seriously overgrown then you could cut it back hard now. You might want to spread the shock to the hedge – and messy work for yourself – over two years, cutting the top and one side back really hard now, and leave the other side until the same time next year. This two-step method is generally a good way to go about the serious renovation of any hedge, incidentally.

Take the opportunity to grub out all the debris from under the hedge, apply a general feed and mulch the root area as well. 🌿

WHITEFLY ALARM

Brian from North Yorkshire describes himself as being in the slough of gardening despond. Having through the winter endured the multiple deaths of major plants – a magnolia and a 10ft (3m) fremontodendron caused him particular pain – he now finds himself 'assaulted' by a plague of whitefly in his conservatory. He has tried every spray available and some he is sure I have never heard of, he says. Absolutely *nothing* works. (By the time I got this far with his lament, I had sussed that end-of-his-tether Brian might just possibly be prone to a touch of fatalistic exaggeration…) Can I help, he sobs?

Glasshouse whitefly present gardeners, particularly impatient ones, with a huge challenge, because they breed so rapidly in hot and steamy greenhouse and conservatory conditions. Mildly afflicted gardeners simply grow a pot or two of pungent yellow tagetes in their greenhouses to keep whitefly at bay (it does work); others routinely hang yellow sticky traps around the place – the yellow attracts insects, the glue immobilises and kills them (beneficial ones as well as the nasties, unfortunately, and do watch out for your hair – been there, stuck to that…). I suggest that once Brian has repelled his whitefly 'assault' to a degree using sticky traps, the best idea (having first removed the traps) would be to then introduce a tiny parasitic wasp, harmless to humans (*Encarsia formosa*) to gobble up the next lot of white-fledglings in his greenhouse. Encarsia are available via mail order from companies that sell biological controls, including Green Gardener and Harrod Horticultural.

Am I really to believe that Brian has tried every single spray available and that absolutely nothing worked? Those sprays suitable for edible crops and herbs, based on fatty acids, plant oils and pyrethrum, for example, as well as the chemical contact insecticides, certainly need repeated applications, and are considered less effective than the systemic chemicals available. The soil drench Provado Vine Weevil Killer 2, which gets into the plant via leaves or roots and makes them unpalatable to pests, works very well, but takes a week or so to 'work properly'.

BROWNING ACER LEAVES

I have a golden-leaved **Acer shirasawanum** *'Aureum' that has started to develop dry, brown blotches on its uppermost leaves, which are also yellower and generally less healthy-looking than those on its lower branches. This is my third*

attempt at growing one of these lovely trees and they keep fading away on me. I am wondering if the site is too sunny, since a tree in the neighbouring garden has been severely cut back this year. Is there anything I can do to save the day?
David, by email

I think your diagnosis of the cause of the leaf blotches is spot-on. All trees or shrubs with golden leaves will scorch or bleach out if grown in full sunlight; other common examples of this are golden philadelphus (*P. coronarius* 'Aureus') and *Choisya ternata* 'Sundance'. This, coupled with the fact that many ornamental Japanese acers, whose natural habitat is under the canopy of larger deciduous trees and which have very thin, papery, wind- and weather-sensitive leaves anyway, means that your young tree is going to struggle.

Even though the large neighbouring tree will eventually thicken up and provide a little more shade, I think that ideally you should move your tree to an even more sheltered site if you can find one. I think it would be risky to do it now, while it is in leaf, so you will have to keep your fingers crossed until the autumn and perform the delicate operation then, when a little root disturbance is unlikely to cause problems. 🌿

LAWN DEVASTATION

Martin had noticed magpies pecking at his lawn and pulling up tufts just before he went away on holiday, but when he returned he found a scene of utter destruction and is now at his wits' end. If so much damage was done simply by birds, exactly what was it they were after?

The birds were undoubtedly after chafer grubs – fat white C-shaped grubs similar to but, at ¾in (1.5cm), much larger than vine weevil grubs, and with distinct legs. In August they hatch out from eggs laid in the ground earlier in the summer and for a month or two they feast on roots, most often grass roots. Infested turf turns dry-looking and if you tug at it lightly the top growth comes away in your hand. Birds are quick to spot the tell-tale signs that chafer grubs are at work, and the combination of feasting grubs, banqueting birds and absentee garden owners can be, as Martin discovered, devastating.

Martin would do well to apply a biological control using nematodes that will destroy a lot of the remaining grubs now, while the soil is warm (above 54°F/12°C) and before they go down deep into the ground for the winter. Chafer Grub Killer from Nemasys is widely available via mail order. It is thoroughly wildlife, people and pet friendly.

RESCUED PLANTS

In answer to Jenny's request as to how she should deal with a trio of 'burnt out' coreopsis plants that she acquired recently from a nursery that was closing down: perennials that have 'gone over' at garden centres are a fairly good bet, and are most often being sold off at this time of year because they no longer look attractive and the manager needs the space. You just transfer them into pots one size larger, inspect them for lurking snails and any other pests, water them with Maxicrop Original Seaweed Extract (Plant Growth Stimulant) or equivalent and they will perk up and sometimes even flower for you in a month's time. But it pays to be wary of seriously cut-price shrubs – getting them back from the brink is not easy (see 'Bargain' Plants, page 91).

SHOTHOLE DISEASE

Our ornamental prunus (Prunus × subhirtella 'Autumnalis'), planted by us some 20 years ago, started to show signs of shothole disease three summers ago and this problem has not gone away. A few weeks ago we removed all the dead branches and twigs and it looks a whole lot better. We then

removed a circular space around the tree and gave it a
hefty feed followed by a slow hose-drench. Is there a cure
and can we save our beautiful tree?
Frank, by email

Shothole disease is another name for bacterial canker or
rather, for the signs of the disease, which manifest themselves
as little holes on the leaves of certain trees and shrubs. It
sounds as though you have done almost all you can possibly
do for this tree and indeed turf removal and feed is a good
idea for any ailing or slow-growing tree. Your tree has, in fact,
reached quite a ripe old age for an ornamental prunus, and
although shothole disease is not necessarily fatal, once an old
tree like yours has the disease and starts dying back seriously,
it is probably on the slippery slide towards eventual death.
You can, of course, fight on. Any further cutting out of dead
or damaged branches should be done when the tree is at its
most vigorous (July, August), as you have done this year.
Spraying the whole tree with a copper-based fungicide (such
as Bordeaux Mixture from Vitax) in the early autumn may
be impractical, because of its size.

As soon as the tree causes more sleepless nights than it
should, and ceases to be properly 'ornamental', if I were you
I would take it out, purely on the grounds that gardening is
intended to be pleasurable – and the results of our labours
are supposed to look attractive. But then, I suspect I have a
reputation for being a bit brutal when advising other people
about what they should take out of their gardens. For the
owners of much-loved landmarks, especially those that
they have planted themselves, giving up is never easy. 🍃

LEMANGE OR ORMON?

Kate sent me a picture of her ten-year-old orange tree – an orange tree
with a difference. It has had a good life to date, spending the winter in

her sun lounge and the rest of the year outside. It rewards her by producing very small oranges all year round. Imagine her surprise when she noticed a small crop of lemons maturing on one of its lower branches. What has caused this, she asks?

It is all about grafting. The ornamental orange must have been grafted on to the root of a more vigorous lemon, and the branch that carries the lemons has come from a bud growing from that root. This sort of thing happens a lot with roses that are grafted on to wild rose rootstock, of course, but I had not seen it on a citrus bush before. As with the roses, the lemon may turn out to be more vigorous than the orange. However, if I were Kate I would do nothing, revel in the curiosity factor, and just see what happens.

CITRUS PEEL AND COMPOST BINS

Why are we so often told that citrus fruit should not be added to compost bins? I have always composted a significant amount of grapefruit, orange and lemon skins apparently without any problem. The compost turns out pretty well, and is pH neutral.
Peter, by email

I had a look at various online gardening forums before I tackled this question – it seems that there are all sorts of opposing views on the matter. Some concerned gardeners claim that any citrus in the compost is a serious no-no, that it kills vital composting worms; some claim that the peel makes the compost too acid and that when it is spread around it will harm your garden soil; also there were odd mutterings about pesticides used on citrus being harmful, etc, etc. (You have to sift through the information on some gardening forums quite carefully to find the helpful nuggets, as you can imagine.)

Citrus peel only really becomes a problem in a wormery – a virtually sealed environment where worms are responsible for all the hard work (see April, page 28). They don't like it if conditions in their work place get too acidic, so those in the habit of adding a lot of citrus and other fruit peelings to the wormery should also add something called Anti-Acid Lime Mix every few weeks (available from Wiggly Wigglers), which helps adjust the pH in there.

In conventional compost bins and heaps, where there are other forces at work in addition to worms (such as bacteria, fungi, etc), it is really a question of adding citrus in moderation and chopping it beforehand. Basically, if things get too acidic (or too hot or too wet), the worms will scarper anyway. So, to sum up: citrus is OK in moderation in a balance of ingredients. ❧

SPRING-FLOWERING SHRUB RESCUE

A Spiraea 'Snowmound', planted a few years ago as part of a shrubby border, is gradually become larger and larger and is starting to nudge out its neighbours. I know it should be pruned when it has finished flowering, but I never get to it before my husband, who recently took the shears to it (à la topiary) and made it look hideous. Advice (that I can wave under his nose) would be welcome.
Sybil, by email

I can understand completely why this pretty, late spring/early summer-flowering shrub is taking over. It flowers at a time when there is a lot going on in the garden that needs our attention and the dense nature of its growth means that new shoots destined to bear the following year's flowers quickly hide the branches of old flowers that should be pruned out.

I suggest, however, that you have a go at breaking the cycle of neglect and 'lollipop' pruning and you (yes, you) can do it now. Get in under there with a pruning saw and secateurs and you will see that there is quite a lot of dead and unproductive wood within the thicket that you can saw out at the base. As you drag these substantial branches out you will see that half the renovation pruning job is done already, so the rest of the operation is quite straightforward: cut down the rest of the bush to a point about a foot or so below the height you want the shrub to be. Surprisingly, although you will then have removed just about all the greenery, there will be one or two young shoots remaining and these will rapidly be joined over the rest of the summer by a new crop of bright shoots – so many that you may want to thin them out a little. It should go without saying that such radical pruning should be followed up with a feed and mulch. The new growth may not flower much next year, but the whole bush will be an absolute picture the following year and of course much easier to prune as long as you get in there quickly with the secateurs before He reaches for the shears. ☙

DISFIGURED ASTRANTIA LEAVES

Janine from Herefordshire was disappointed that the leaves of her *Astrantia major* were irregularly blotched this year. The perpetrator of this nuisance disfigurement is a fly called *Phytomyza astrantiae*, which, as the name suggests, is host-specific. The fly punctures the leaves to lay its eggs, and it is the tiny grubs that hatch and feed within the leaf tissue that cause the patches. The flies arrive in April or May, so a systemic spray (Provado Ultimate Bug Killer) of the young astrantia foliage at that time will go some way to preventing the problem. Astrantias re-flower if they are cut right back in late summer. So Janine could also spray the new leaves that are forthcoming now, in the hope that they will stay 'clean'.

WASPS

By now the problem will have already resolved itself, but I can reassure Sue that wasps do not nest in the same place two years running. However, the presence of fruit trees in her garden pretty much ensures that they will find a place nearby to make a nest next year.

DOROTHY PERKINS – TOO LONG IN THE TOOTH?

I have a climbing rose – 'Dorothy Perkins' – that has a very serious case of mildew. It had it last year and I sprayed it, fed it and failed to control it. This year it is worse than ever. Is there anything I can do, or do I have to admit defeat and dig it up?
Penny, by email

It may give you and Josie from Loughborough, who has a similar problem, some comfort to know that this pretty rose is notoriously disease-prone. It is one of a group of climbing roses with an unusually long flowering season known as Wichurana ramblers, introduced at the very start of the nineteenth century. Old roses such as these do not have disease resistance bred into them in the same way as more modern introductions, and it shows.

The war of attrition with roses that are known to get bad mildew has to start early in the season, since while prevention is possible, a real cure is far less so. And it is no good imagining that a single treatment with a systemic fungicide or one of the systemic rose insecticide/fungicide cocktails will do the trick. You have to repeat the performance every few weeks – possibly, if I dare be so bold, a little more often than the manufacturer's instructions tell you – right through the season.

Good cultivation helps too: judicious pruning to keep the growth open and uncongested. As does feeding with a proper rose fertiliser in spring and again just after mid-summer, as well as conscientious mulching. So should you dig poor old Dorothy up? Possibly, if the rose is growing in cramped conditions against a hot brick wall – a situation in which most roses would succumb easily to disease. But I hate advising people to dig up roses, it goes against the grain. And what would go in its place? Better the devil, etc – and this one is a rather pretty devil. 🌿

WISTERIA DEATH

Geoff is one of a regular stream of readers writing to me about mysterious failure of their wisteria. Is there a new disease going around? No, but here, briefly, are some common causes of failure of this apparently must-have climber (which in my opinion is potentially far too big and too high maintenance for most of the places in which it is planted).

1. Non-flowering occurs if plants are still young. (It may take ten or even 20 years for a non-grafted plant to flower, so if in doubt, plant one that is grafted and has evidence of flowers.)

2. Flowers on established plants fail because of random bird attacks, sharp frost, or even extremes of day/night temperature when buds are about to open.

3. Whole plants die back because of a) honey fungus, b) phytophthora – a potentially fatal fungal disease prevalent where roots are frequently winter waterlogged, c) sudden failure of the graft union near the base of the plant (in which case growth might eventually come from below the graft), d) infestation of sap-sucking wisteria scale – large ½in (1cm) dome-shaped 'limpets'; rare, confined as yet to London area.

FIRST GARDENING STEPS

Zarah loves purple and has just bought two beautifully flowering lavender plants to adorn the balcony of the flat in East London where she lives. How can she keep them alive as long as possible, she asks? Raise not an eyebrow, ye green-fingered regulars – from such balcony beginnings mighty gardeners are made. Trim the flowers and stalks off when they have finished, Zarah. Transfer the little plants into pots one or two sizes larger, using a soil-based compost (called John Innes No 2), and water them to settle them in. Then put them somewhere on the balcony where they won't be forgotten and dry out completely or sit in a puddle all winter (which would kill them) and will be sheltered from frost (ditto: you don't want the roots to freeze solid). They will start growing again in March. Enjoy. Try kitchen herbs next year as well.

VARIOUS SHADES OF GREY

Fenella really likes her felty-grey-leaved *Senecio* 'Sunshine' (actually now re-named *Brachyglottis* 'Sunshine'), planted some years ago by the previous owners of her garden in an only partially sunny place, but doesn't like the yellow flowers that presumably give it its name. Each summer she snips out the flower buds before they open, and now that the shrub has reached mammoth proportions, this takes a lot of time and effort. Is there another grey-leaved shrub that will survive in similar conditions?

Not really. Almost all grey- and felty-leaved shrubs that we grow here need a lot of sun together with poor, free-draining soil – most being natives of the Mediterranean region or dry rocky hills of Asia Minor. In less than these ideal conditions they become stringy, floppy and don't flower well. The reason brachyglottis became so popular is that it breaks all the grey-leaved plant rules and will happily grow – rather too well in many cases – in semi-shade and averagely fertile garden soil. But it is almost universally looked on with slight disapproval because of its untidy yellow flowers, too reminiscent of a distantly related weed, ragwort.

I feel, however, that before she rolls up her sleeves and gets out her spade, Fenella should try to manipulate this shrub into non-flowering or minimal-flowering submission by pruning it. Instead of just taking off the flowers or buds as they appear next year, she should give the shrub a massive prune in mid-spring. And I do mean massive. By reducing it to a woody framework about 28in (70cm) in all directions, taking off huge amounts of by now gnarled old growth, leaving just stumps with perhaps a few tiny leafy shoots in evidence, she will just about stop it flowering. For a mere three weeks or so, the plant will be, I admit, unsightly. But re-growth will be so rapid that by August it will be re-clothed in its pristine ever-grey foliage. Coincidentally I did this to an overgrown brachyglottis in my own garden, and took the opportunity to plant some large white annual tobacco plants in the space created. These are now flowering in amongst – and supported by – the renewed grey foliage of a completely flowerless brachyglottis and even though I say it as shouldn't, it was a rather inspired idea and they do look rather good.

A SMALL, PRETTY GARDEN TREE

I am looking for a pretty tree that will have blossom and/or fruit and autumn colour, and which does not grow much higher than 13–16ft (4–5m). I would like a tree that has a straight stem for approx 6½ft (2m) and then a canopy. This is with a view to hiding my neighbour's roof (which is pretty ugly). My fence is 6½ft (2m) high. Am I looking for the holy grail?
Daphne, by email

No, I don't think you are looking for the holy grail: I instantly thought of an amelanchier, possibly the best small-garden tree. It has white-ish early spring blossom followed by fluttery leaves that are translucent pink but quickly turn green and then colour fabulously in the autumn, at which time, if the birds leave them alone, you become aware of small maroon fruits. The leaves, being quite small, form a canopy that is not too dense, nor does the tree get too large, probably growing to 13–16ft (4–5m) or so in 10–15 years. Otherwise, have you considered a winter-flowering prunus (*P.* × *subhirtella* 'Autumnalis'), which has a lovely, airy, lightweight summer canopy after flushes of winter flowers? Neither of these is a particularly fast grower, so you should start with as decent a sized tree as you can manhandle and afford. Elsewhere in your letter you mentioned a birch (also a good choice, but they do get quite tall), and there are some lovely hawthorns (*Crataegus persimilis* 'Prunifolia' has particularly good autumn colour) and crab apple trees (such as *Malus floribunda*) that have intense blossom and fruit.

Now is the time to visit a tree nursery, while everything is at least in leaf, to make a shortlist or even a decision, and reserve a tree to plant in the autumn. 🌿

UPRIGHT CITIZENS

Here are four bomb-proof herbaceous plants that will stand tall whatever the weather, without any help from you – no staking, propping or leaning on neighbouring plants.

Hemerocallis (day lilies) The wishy-washy orange variety has fallen out of favour for reasons of ubiquity in older gardens. But there are scores of more interesting varieties – 'Stafford' is dark-flowered, easy to source.

Aconitum 'Arendsii' (monkshood) At 4ft (1.2m) tall this is a back-of-the border plant favoured by those with gardens too exposed for delphiniums. Bolt upright with no help whatsoever (see also September, pages 119 and 121).

Astrantia major (masterwort) Best variety is 'Shaggy' (a.k.a. 'Margery

Fish'). Lovely green-tipped white lacy flowers on firm 3ft (90cm) stems. Bonus point: repeats in autumn if you cut it back.

Euphorbia palustris (marsh spurge) A strong, clumpy, 3ft (90cm) tall herbaceous spurge with leaves that turn a good autumn yellow. Dislikes extremely arid soil but 'marsh' not obligatory.

THINGS TO CONSIDER IN AUGUST

✿ Camellias start to make flower buds this month. Make sure they don't lack water at this stage or they may disappoint next spring.

✿ Big border phlox and *Campanula lactiflora* benefit from gentle deadheading. Smaller buds will be already waiting lower down their stems and will provide a little colour in the following weeks. And most verbascum cultivars will produce fresh (but shorter) flower spikes if their 'primaries' are cut down now.

✿ Cut down sweet pea plants that have finished flowering, but leave their roots in the soil for a few weeks – they will add nitrogen.

✿ Mow or scythe wildflower meadows and mini-meadows and rake up the dry remains once they have dropped their seed. Keep the grass short thereafter.

Secateurs at the ready
✿ Cut yew and holly hedges and prune other evergreens. Photinia will make new red shoots that will brighten the garden in early autumn.

✿ Trim back unwanted shoots of evergreen star jasmine (*Trachelospermum*) if it needs to be controlled. It can be pruned again in spring and will flower on its new growth next summer.

✿ As lavender finishes flowering, trim bushes all over to create a neat shape, removing old flowers and their stalks, plus an inch or two of foliage beneath.

✹ This month you have a last chance to lightly prune *Clematis montana* without spoiling next year's flower power.

✹ Deadhead climbers and bush roses, and prune once-flowering shrub roses, cutting back the shoots that have just done their thing, preserving the new ones now clearly visible.

Pests and diseases
✹ Don't take your eye off the ball as far as mildew and blackspot on roses are concerned (as well as rust on hollyhocks) – this is the month when fungal diseases can take hold. Spray with systemic fungicide, clear up fallen leaves, and tweak blighted leaves off hollyhock stems.

✹ Drench soil in containers with Nemasys Vine Weevil Killer, a biological (i.e. non-chemical) treatment to knobble the destructive root-munching grubs of this black, snouty beetle.

✹ On hot days look out for sap-sucking leafhoppers whizzing around rhododendrons (only obvious if you shake the bushes). They spread the fungal disease bud blast which causes blackened bristly flower buds that fail to open. Spray with a systemic insecticide.

Autumn

September

TAKING OFF THE BLINKERS

The more time we spend in our gardens with our heads in our borders, the more likely we are to acquire blinkers that stop us seeing them clearly. The problems are frequently the results of our first efforts. Even real gardeners who shun 'instant' may find themselves whacking in a few big plants – applying bold brushstrokes to an otherwise blank canvas. All too often these bolder plants reward us by gradually taking over, casting shade, mopping up all the moisture in the soil, obliterating views and squeezing out other, more delicate newcomers – while we are so busy fiddling with the detail of it all that we just don't notice.

We all, to a certain extent, have the same problem – even those with the most go-ahead and toiled-over gardens. Years ago I noticed that the droves of visitors to a frightfully famous place not far from where I live always made a beeline (and still do) for a strategically placed bench at the end of the magnificent long mixed border, to survey it from its 'best' angle. The gorgeous half-timbered house forms a mellow backdrop to the entire garden, but from this particular vantage point the view of it was totally obscured by a dense, mop-headed tree. It was almost as if someone had put a muddy thumbprint bang in the middle of a beautiful artwork.

It has occurred to me since that I may have completely missed the point: the tree was probably deliberately placed and allowed to grow to its considerable size, the illustrious owner (now no longer with us) finding the sight of ever present rows of anoraked visitors, perched on his bench like a row of stunned wood pigeons, a less-than-lovely embellishment to the view of his truly wonderful acreage from within the house.

I apologise for this somewhat rambling piece, the point of which is to remind readers to take time to look at their gardens with their blinkers off. Every so often, and certainly at least once a year, we should all go and sit where we like to sit and see if we are seeing what we want to see, indeed what we originally intended to see, and, if not, do something about it. By subtly raising the canopies of trees, by more (or less) rigorous pruning or even complete removal of things that were planted in the early days as quick fixes, we can re-open little views and vistas and give our gardens a refreshing shot in the arm. Remember also that friends who visit our gardens are not similarly blinkered (they have a different pair which they pop on as soon as they get home), and their candid observations can actually point us in new directions – even though we may instinctively smart at their presumptuousness.

Practise what you preach, they say, and when reviewing the above for inclusion here, I decided that in this instance I more or less do. I now take regular un-blinkered looks at the state of play on my own little pitch, home to several huge trees and (because I love them) probably too many shrubs. I have the trees thinned out and keep tabs on the size of any shrubs that threaten seriously to limit the amount of sun that reaches my borders. I like to think I am keeping on top of everything. But doubtless there is a lot more I still can't and don't see.

UPSIDE DOWN OR DOWNSIDE UP?

I planted some roughly saucer-shaped cyclamen corms with their concave sides uppermost and their rounded sides facing downwards. My wife says that is the wrong way up and that the 'saucer' side will collect water and rot. Who is right?
John, Sutton, Greater London

You are. But they are not actually corms, they are tubers. 🌿

NOT SO ANGELIC

A few years ago I bought some yellow archangel plants at a church fair. I wanted to fill a rather uninteresting corner of the garden. The plants have thrived to say the least and are spreading quickly into other areas. I am concerned, however, that I may be cultivating a problem plant.
Jennifer, by email

You have indeed invited a hooligan to the party without knowing it. Variegated yellow archangel, a.k.a. yellow deadnettle or *Lamium galeobdolon*, is an utterly enchanting hedgerow plant most noticeable in early spring, with its silver-motley leaves and perfectly vertical short spires of lemon-yellow flowers, lighting up areas of deep shade where little else will grow. What a gift to a gardener, you might think. Not. Yellow archangel does not know when to stop and can cover 100 square metres in three to five years. It is now regarded here as a serious countryside weed that obliterates just about everything in its path. The only good thing about this is the fact that it will completely out-thug that much uglier garden horror – ground elder.

What now, you ask? Selectively rip and burn, or at very least carefully isolate a small patch each year, and don't let it get the upper hand. Don't lob bits over the hedge into the countryside and don't pot up bits for the church fair. 🌿

AUTUMN LAWNS: THREE BIRDS, ONE STONE

If you are going to do so, now is probably the best time to get fussy and, with a bit of clever planning, it need not involve too much drudgery. Hopefully the ground is reasonably damp and still warm – ideal for a gentle bit of aeration, top-dressing, autumn feeding and re-seeding.
1. Start by gently raking the lawn to 'raise the pile' and tease out the weaker plantlets, general debris and some of the moss.

2. Then mow it quite short (because you don't want to mow it again for a while). Don't compost the collected mowings: moss doesn't rot down, and you will risk spreading it around your borders via your compost.

3. Next, spike the lawn, or at least any compacted areas, with a garden fork, repeatedly sticking it in the turf as far as you can and wiggling it around before pulling it out again. Better still, borrow a hollow-tine aerator, which actually takes out plugs of soil, which can then be swept up.

4. Follow this by putting some commercially bagged turf dressing (also referred to as top dressing, see April, page 29) in a wheelbarrow.

5. Into the barrow of turf dressing also mix approximately a generous fistful of grass seed (try RHS Supreme Green Lawn Seed with Rootgrow mycorrhizal fungi) per spadeful of dressing. Clever mathematicians might also be able to work out how much autumn lawn feed could be added to this, thus killing three birds with one stone.

6. Dump two spadefuls of the magic mixture per square metre on the lawn and, using a stiff broom, brush it evenly around into an extremely thin layer. Some of it will hopefully drop down, or will eventually get naturally washed down, into the holes created by the aeration and so improve the quality of the turf.

7. Those who were not clever mathematicians can apply the autumn lawn feed at this point. It is worth remembering that the application of an autumn feed (which benefits the roots, but does not make the grass grow) does not need to be nearly as precise as the spring/summer ones.

If we have a mild autumn and the grass continues to grow, mow rarely and keep the mower on a high setting.

The considerable benefits of all this hard work may not be apparent till next summer.

TALES OF INFESTATION

Angela wonders what she should do with the contents of a previous owner's enormous compost bin that is absolutely infested with weed seeds – she found this frustrating fact out when innocently using it as a general soil improver earlier in the year. In her situation I would use the compost only where I could bury it deeply – when trench-digging veg beds or making new borders, for example. Or I would use it to improve soil underneath individual new plantings of herbaceous plants and shrubs. The weed seeds won't/can't germinate if they are far enough underground and unlikely to be exposed to light.

THE LIGHT FANTASTIC

You have to play the hand you are dealt as best you can in gardening, as in everything. Not only have I learnt not to beat myself up about my short-sighted weakness for mid-summer floral extravagance, but I have adopted a different attitude to the areas of my garden where the shade cast by its numerous trees creeps up on you by late August. I now quite deliberately plant to take advantage of exactly where and in what way the late-day light falls on sunny days as summer fades.

Plants with translucent foliage – most specifically the reds – are strategically placed so as to be back-lit by the increasingly golden sunlight. *Cercis canadensis* 'Forest Pansy', already starting to colour up, its plum-coloured leaves turning yellow, orange and scarlet in stages, becomes gloriously illuminated by the September sun that slants under an enormous oak and slices across the garden from the west, lighting up two weighty clumps of persicaria: *P.* 'Red Dragon', its leaves and stems splashed vivid red, and *P. amplexicaulis* 'Taurus', whose fine, pointed vermilion candles smoulder for weeks.

Elsewhere, rusty rodgersias glow darkly along with the ripening seeds of a maroon-red angelica, the whole collection enlivened in late afternoon by sunlight on the adjacent bright cream-striped leaves of *Miscanthus* 'Cosmopolitan' and by clusters of lipstick-scarlet hips of a feral rose clambering through the hazel that overhangs the pond. The

117

whole garden seems laced through with glowing red at this time. On a trellis by the entrance, *Cotinus* 'Grace' in full ruby-red sail almost out-shines the huge show-off pots of deep red dahlias that flank the gate. The cotinus is the dominant player in a vibrant tangle that includes the prematurely reddening extremities of *Parthenocissus quinquefolia* and the jewel-like scarlet berries of *Viburnum opulus*.

I am a bit of a sucker for translucency generally – and not just of red things. I even cull my white honesty (*Lunaria annua* var. *albiflora*) colony, allowing to set seed only a few plants that are in the right place to catch the last rays. And then, of course, the true obsessive that I am, I spend far too much time (when I should be writing) gently easing off the outer dull grey discs of their seed heads to reveal their opaque, mother-of-pearl perfection that will, I know, be ruined all too soon by the first of the autumn gales.

LATE COLOURS

Emailer Faith, 'not a very clever gardener', she says, bemoans the fact that her garden looks pretty in spring and early summer but gradually goes downhill, with hardly any flowers to cheer her into autumn. Have I any suggestions?

This colourless end-of-season wind-down is, in my experience, an incredibly common problem, fuelled by the fact that a lot of gardeners tend to have only two serious Moments of Zeal. The first typically results in the buying of scores of bulbs in September to cheer the garden in spring. The second, in spring/early summer – itself a time when it is easy to overlook late-flowering perennials which may look virtually moribund in their pots then – is when they go instead for young (tunnel-raised) high summer perennials, prematurely in flower and looking luscious but vulnerable and destined to 'burn out' rather early. And of course there is a tendency to buy oceans of summer bedding and container plants for almost instant gratification.

The best way, therefore, to inject late colour into your garden is to get your fork stuck into border work early in the autumn to take advantage of what is on offer at nurseries and autumn plant fairs (where everything is sold in full flower). My own borders don't really bear close examination, admittedly, but there is still plenty going on... and on (see 'The Light Fantastic', above). It may help Faith if I simply mention just some of these plants that are still holding their own.

While there are some important asters (*A.* × *frikartii* 'Mönch', *A. novae-angliae* 'Harrington's Pink', *A. divaricatus*) and grasses (*Miscanthus nepalensis*, *M.* 'Cosmopolitan' are the best here), there are other flowers still blazing away. Most brilliant are a deep purple/blue *Aconitum* 'Arendsii' (see August, page 107, and A Delphinium Lookalike, page 121), *Salvia patens* (a slightly tender perennial, grown from seed this year and not expected to overwinter). Yellow daisies *Inula hookeri*, and lofty, back-of-the-border *Helianthus* 'Lemon Queen' are looking good. Dahlias in large containers (easier to keep snailfree than when they are in the ground) were late to get going and thus are at their peak. Japanese anemones are just coming to an end, but dusky-blue *Calamintha nepeta* and various maroon-flowered marjorams are still hazily pretty and some cut-back astrantias are having another go. Geraniums 'Ann Folkard' and 'Rozanne' are still sprawling around through everything, miles from home.

Most surprisingly, phlox that had their top flower heads trimmed back a month or more ago have produced some little flowers lower down their stems, so there are welcome glimmers of pink and mauve in the borders here and there. Shrubs? The hydrangeas and hardy fuchsias are still magnificent, benefitting from the wet spring, no doubt, while Modern Shrub roses are having a last hot flush. A shrub to be thoroughly recommended for its late pretty performance is *Abelia* × *grandiflora*. Finally, let's hear it for my delinquents: a barely controlled messy swarm of pot marigolds, cut back to the bone a month ago, is putting on a blistering late show, as is *Verbena bonariensis* that annually pops up around the place uninvited.

POSTSCRIPT: Loads of readers wrote in with late summer flower suggestions based on what was giving a grand finale in their own gardens as late as October.

So thank you Hugh, Diana, Molly, Adam, Maggie, Audrey, Alex, Marion, Jo, Teresa and (another) Faith for the following:

Abutilon megapotamicum

Cosmos

Osteospermum

Sedums

Nasturtiums

Kniphofia

Chrysanthemums

Rudbeckia fulgida var. *sullivantii* 'Goldsturm'

Cyclamen coum

Salvia microphylla (various)

Penstemons

WISTERIA FROM SEED?

Brian's six-year-old grafted wisteria has produced what looks like a giant seed pod. Does it contain viable seeds, and should he try to grow another plant from it? Yes, he can certainly grow another plant from a seed within the pod. It may not be identical to the 'parent' plant, and the problem with wisteria seedlings – as so many people have discovered who bought a seedling plant rather than seeking out a grafted plant – is that they take many years to grow to flowering size: up to a decade.

Maybe Brian has grandchildren who would benefit from his efforts…

MICHAELMAS DAISY NO-SHOW

Jill's Michaelmas daisies (*Aster novi-belgii*), planted five years ago, did not flower this year for the first time. The picture she sent me showed a very sad forest of flowerless stems, the bottom two-thirds of which were clothed with drab, dry, brown leaves. Apart from a sunless summer, three other possibilities or indeed a combination of all of them could be the cause. This kind of aster is the very devil for mildew when under stress (varieties of *Aster amellus* or *A. novae-angliae* or *A. divaricatus* suffer far less). So after four years the plant needs splitting or at least lifting and replanting with bonemeal and lots of moisture-retaining compost around its feet. From Jill's picture I couldn't detect puckered, pin-pricked shoot tips, which would have indicated a late summer capsid bug onslaught that would also have prevented flowering.

A DELPHINIUM LOOKALIKE

In late September on holiday on the Isle of Wight I saw a magnificent plant in a garden that I first thought was a delphinium. It had tall stems with leaves that looked similar to delphinium leaves, and black-centred flowers that also looked similar, although each one seemed to have an extra petal – like a hat – on top. What was it?
Terry, by email

From your description, it was an aconitum – most probably *Aconitum* 'Arendsii'. Aconitums belong to the same family as delphiniums and are a large group of mostly perennial, purple or creamy-white-flowered garden plants, some performing earlier in the summer, others rather usefully not putting on a show until September and October. The strange hooded flowers have given them the common name of monkshood. Their leaves are somewhat coarse. Some have shorter stems and more open flower panicles, others have tapering spires of flowers and indeed are easy to mistake for delphiniums if seen from afar.

There are several great things about monkshood of which many gardeners may be unaware. The first is that they are totally, wonderfully, unattractive to slugs and snails, unlike their notoriously tasty relations. Secondly, their stems (particularly of the variety that you espied on your travels) are thicker and sturdier than delphiniums and most of them do not need the intricate and tiresome support system that delphiniums demand. Thirdly, they grow well in shady places. What a fabulous group of plants, you might say, why doesn't everyone grow them?

There is, of course, a (minor) drawback, and monkshoods have somewhat failed to find a place in the hearts of many gardeners in the way that delphiniums have because a) the foliage can be mildly irritant to the skin, and b) all parts of the plants are poisonous if ingested. The 'irritant to the skin' part of the caveat is relatively easy to deal with once you know about it; many of us grow 'irritant' plants (such as euphorbias, for example) – we just take care when gardening around them. Personally I look somewhat sideways at the 'toxic if ingested' label on plants – unless they happen to closely resemble a specific food crop, perhaps. I know of no one daft enough to wade into their borders and graze on their perennials, do you? 🌾

LILY BULBILS

My lilies have produced small grape-like nodules
underneath each leaf on the stems. I am wondering
what they are and whether I can propagate from them.
Can you help?
M N, Mablethorpe, Lincolnshire

These are known as bulbils and you can certainly have a go at propagating from them. I should say that not all lilies produce these bulbils – some produce tiny bulblets around the base of the stems at soil level, which can be separated and grown on to form mature plants, and you can propagate all lilies by removing individual 'scales' from the adult bulbs (much as you would propagate garlic).

What would happen naturally, were you to leave the stems and bulbils alone, is that the bulbils would drop to the ground as the stems started to brown and die and those few that survived the winter intact would then start to produce roots and would eventually become bulbs in their own right – a bit of a hit and miss process. If you want to be sure of getting new bulbs (which will not necessarily be identical to the 'parent' lily, incidentally), you could cut the stems down now and remove the bulbils, pressing them gently into the surface of sandy cuttings compost in a seed tray and covering them with a layer of fine grit. Keep the seed tray somewhere frost free and the bulbils will start to make tiny leaves in the spring. When they are large enough to be handled, you could carefully plant them in large pots of more gutsy loam-based compost in twos and threes, or alternatively you can try to plant the contents of the seed tray intact into a garden border, thereby potentially creating a ready-made clump of lilies. They will probably take two years to flower. ❦

SEEING RED

Ken and Sue want to plant a hedge 'with a bit of interest', and have come across photinia and pieris. Are they one and the same thing?

There is a huge difference. Photinia is a large shrub that will grow to 8ft (2.4m) or more in five years (the best variety is 'Red Robin'), producing red leaf shoots in spring that then turn green. It will shoot red again in the summer if it is lightly pruned. If left un-pruned, it will flower from shoot tips (in white-ish sprays). Photinia copes with light shade and makes a good evergreen hedging shrub mixed with others (pink-budded *Viburnum tinus* is one, *Rhamnus alaternus* 'Argenteovariegata' is another).

Pieris is a woodland shub that dislikes exposure and needs leafy acid soil. It is slow growing, some varieties reaching 8ft (2.4m) in 20 years but many are much smaller. Pieris bears scented drooping sprays of white or pink flowers in spring, and many varieties carry scarlet bracts that gradually fade to green (hence the superficial similarity to photinia). It does not respond well to pruning and is not really a hedging plant. It looks best amongst other woodlanders – azaleas and so on.

WHIFFS AND BUTTS

We have two garden sheds that have the same materials on their roofs and each has a water butt. One of them always gives us clean water whilst the other, despite bi-annual cleaning, only produces smelly, frothy, slightly green water. It is quite near an oak tree, so is this the cause? How can we produce clean water without adding chemicals?
Joan, by email

I have no doubt that the oak tree is the main cause of your problem here. Organic matter of any kind that gets into water butts will rot and make the water smell evil, and I suspect that the gutters of the shed near the oak are getting clogged with oak leaves, many of which are finding their way into the problem water butt. There are various steps you could take. You could put a mesh guard over the entire gutter, or use one of the various gadgets sold to stop leaves going down the downpipe, or put a snippet from an old pair of tights over the end of the downpipe to trap leaves (checking it every so often, even in summer).

I smell another rat here, however. Are your water butts

covered? Lids on water butts keep out not only autumn leaves and other detritus, but also keep out the light, which otherwise allows algae to grow, as well as squadrons of summer mosquitoes. Furthermore, covered butts are a lot less intriguing to inquisitive children and also (sadly I have had this one brought home to me) to thirsty fledgling birds. Finally, there are non-chemical treatments for water butts. You could try Water Butt Treatment by Biotal. ✺

DIVIDING HELLEBORES

We have had a truly wonderful display from our hellebores this year. Some were bought as young plants some four to five years ago and have expanded considerably; others are from self-sown seedlings. Can the larger mature plants be divided? If so, what is the best way to do this, and when?
Mrs J, by email

The picture that accompanied your email did indeed show a mighty and most beautiful colony of hellebores – Oriental hybrids, which make clumps that gradually expand and flower on new shoots in February and March, closely followed by bright new foliage. Multi-coloured colonies like yours are formed over time by self-sown seedlings that take a couple of years, maybe more, to start flowering.

There really is no need to divide your big clumps – they will motor on for years while their 'children' gradually take over more of the stage if suitably fed and mulched. But gardeners with particularly striking coloured plants sometimes prefer to divide them rather than rely on self-seeding, which inevitably seems to result in a gradual dilution – and rather a lot of washed-out coloured plants.

So if you want to divide, do it now in early autumn, when the plants put out a lot of new root growth so recovery will be more or less guaranteed. Do it by digging out the whole clump and carving it up (a certain amount of root damage is inevitable, but won't be fatal at this time). The most productive and vigorous parts of the clump will be the outside sections, as with all clump-forming perennials.

I should perhaps add, for the benefit of other readers, that dividing clumps of other hellebores is not such a great idea. The far trickier-to-establish *H. niger* (Christmas rose) does not settle down easily once disturbed. And those with biennial flower stems, such as *H. × sternii*, do not take kindly to root division at any time of year, so may simply wilt and die. If they are allowed to set seed (an ugly process, involving old shoots heavy with seed pods masking the emergence of the spanking new ones), you may get the odd youngster appearing around the place if you are lucky. ✤

RABBIT DAMAGE

Penelope's lovely witch hazel, *Hamamelis × intermedia* 'Pallida', a gift from her husband three years ago, flowered well this year but, horror of horrors, its bark at the bottom of its stems has now been eaten away by rabbits. Her husband says it will die – but can she not dig it up and replant it deeper to cover the damage or bind something around the stems, she asks? No, I am afraid not. Penelope's husband may be right, alas. Certainly those stems that have had their bark nibbled around their entire circumference will die, so even if it survives, the bush might end up a bit of a strange shape. And replanting more deeply is not the answer – root tissue and stem tissue are quite different, and buried stems would simply rot. Best hope? Clean removal with secateurs of obviously doomed stems. After that, a temporary fence of chicken wire should put off the nibblers – who only relish young stems of woody plants, it would seem, and leave them alone once mature. Rabbit guards to protect lower stems of trees and shrubs are also available at garden centres.

HEAVE HO?

We have a protected, large, very mature walnut tree that is looking very sorry for itself. Two local gardeners have suggested it's at the end of its natural life. This season it leafed very early and, very unusually, is bearing virtually no fruit. We will, of course, consult a local tree surgeon, but are worried that if it does have to come down, it might create problems of heave to three houses that are all about 33ft (10m) from it. You opinion would be most welcome.
David, Lavenham, Suffolk

First, a word about trees 'looking sorry for themselves' – leaf spot and other fungal diseases, premature shedding of leaves, etc, are, unsurprisingly, mostly about the weather, extremes of which seem to upset a lot of trees greatly. Your walnut tree may not be on its last legs, and as you clearly realise you should not necessarily take the opinion of 'two local gardeners' – or me for that matter. You need to seek the opinion of a properly qualified and respected tree surgeon who thoroughly knows his onions. Or perhaps more sensibly, more than one.

As for the possibility of 'heave' if you do have to take the tree out (this is a term given to subsidence caused by the removal or shrinkage of the roots of big trees that have become embedded in building foundations): I have asked tree surgeons about this before, since it seems to be a very real public concern, and have been told that it is generally forest trees – oak, sycamore, etc – that cause the problem, and specifically where seedlings have tucked themselves in extremely close to house walls and been allowed to develop into mighty trees over a substantial number of years. For what it is worth, a walnut tree, 10m from buildings, would not seem to fit into this category. 🌿

'WHISTLING JACKS'

Leaving a B&B in Cornwall, the owner pressed into my hand a paper bag of about 25 bulbs she called 'Whistling Jacks', presuming that I would know exactly what they were. I believe they are a kind of gladioli, but can't find any reference to them in my books.
L K, Birmingham

'Whistling Jack' is the West Country name often given to *Gladiolus communis* subsp. *byzantinus*, a native of the mountain pastures of the eastern Mediterranean as the name suggests, where it flowers in early spring. It grows well here in sheltered places and flowers in May/June, and will naturalise when conditions suit it, as indeed it does in Cornwall. With refined flowers on slender stems, 'Whistling Jacks' are a far cry from the overweight, summer-flowering Dame Edna 'gladdies'. The best ones are a deeply dazzling orange-throated magenta, and those sold from known well-coloured stock tend to be extremely expensive. Regrettably, it would seem that some commercial stocks have become weakened. I bought some a few years ago that turned out to have rather insipid flowers that were less magenta, more a watery shocking pink, so I got rid of them after a year. I should imagine that, since the givers of this lovely gift were clearly very proud of their bulbs, they will be the real McCoy, in which case, lucky you.

Plant them now, somewhere reasonably sheltered, at the base of a warm wall, perhaps, at a depth of about three or four times their height, with a little grit (to ensure good drainage, which they need) and a sprinkle of bonemeal in the soil underneath each. Plant them in informal groups of five or more, a few inches apart, and just leave them well alone for a few years. They look great with self-sown (i.e. early summer-flowering) sky-blue nigella, by the way. As I say, lucky you. ❧

128

THINGS TO CONSIDER IN SEPTEMBER

❉ Don't give up on the deadheading of plants, particularly annuals, that still have more to give.

❉ While the soil is warm and plants have vestiges of leaf and flower, you might as well get on with splitting and replanting.

❉ Snails may already be ceasing activities for the season but big fat slugs are still on the march, demolishing autumn delphinium shoots and any seedlings they come across.

❉ At the end of the month, houseplants that were on holiday outdoors should be brought indoors. Check that no slugs and snails come too.

❉ Treat perennial weeds such as ground elder with a glyphosate weedkiller before they go underground for the winter.

❉ Very gently and gradually bend new upward-reaching shoots of climbing roses into more horizontal positions and secure them.

❉ Spring-flowerers such as alliums, gladioli and daffodils are best planted in September, when they naturally start to make their roots.

Get organised for autumn

❉ A jumbo Bosmere tip bag or plastic sheet and Jakoti shears make border dismantling easier.

❉ Free up a compost bin to receive all the newest border snippings and trimmings by bagging up the contents for later use as a soil-improver.

❉ Make a simple cage for composting leaves – four posts wrapped around with chicken wire and a base of weed-smothering membrane.

❉ Sort out the mess in the shed before the autumn gardening rush.

October

HEAVEN SCENT

My postbag often contains letters from readers who want to grow more scented plants – especially around their patios and favourite seating areas. This is a good time for all of us to think about such things as we go into prime planning and planting time, so here goes.

First let's turn our noses towards the aromatic herbs that fill the air with scent when brushed past or bruised. The obvious players here are the sunny-site familiars: rosemary, thyme, lavender, marjoram and so on. Less well known is *Aloysia citrodora*, a.k.a. lemon verbena, a refined, slightly tender little shrub that produces delicate panicles of flowers around now but is chiefly appreciated for the smell of its intense, citrus-y leaves. It is best grown in a pot and given a bit of winter protection, and should on no account be confused with lemon balm, *Melissa officinalis*, a perennial which is, in my book, an intolerable (and boring-looking) thuggy self-seeder. Not all herbs and aromatics do the right business, however. Steer clear of some of the salvias, of which *S. sclarea* var. *turkestanica*, with its ethereally lovely flowers, is a major offender. 'Sweaty housemaids', my late mother described its pong – though what she actually knew about housemaids I can't imagine, never having employed such a thing in her life and probably not having encountered anyone else's overheated one at close quarters either.

Beautifully scented flowers are numerous. Honeysuckle and annual tobacco plants (nicotiana) are old favourites, of course (of the latter, the varieties *N. alata* and *N. sylvestris* are best), and can be tucked in anywhere. Some of the following may be less well known. One of my favourites is a scented border perennial, *Actaea* (formerly *Cimicifuga*) *simplex*. This produces flowers – tall perfumed white wands – in August. There is a particularly beautiful variety called 'Brunette' with deep chocolate-coloured leaves (that need mid-day dappled shade in high summer, lest they scorch). *Matthiola incana*, the short-lived shrubby perennial stock with architectural rosettes of grey foliage, seeds itself around so that you need never be without it. I always have large containers of it standing around on my tiny terrace and I pot up stray seedlings each year as replacements. A compact, pretty annual, *Zaluzianskya*, fabulously scented at night, seems to be appearing more regularly with the usual run-of-the-mill bedding stuff at garden centres of late – a pot of it is heavenly in the centre of a garden table, but needs regular deadheading and high-potash feeding or it gives up flowering by late summer. The evergreen climber *Trachelospermum jasminoides* has a long-ish flowering season and should by now be familiar to most readers (heaven knows, I have sung its praises enough), and for autumn/early winter scent (similar to that of lily of the valley – which is another early summer goodie no one should be without), a single plant or hedge of evergreen *Elaeagnus pungens* 'Maculata' can't be beaten. Far less well known is a late-flowering deciduous shrub, *Cestrum parqui*, which carries pretty clusters of lime-green flowers that can surprise you with their sweet-shop whiff on a mild autumn evening.

Finally, a reminder that we don't all 'get' everything in the same way – far from it, in fact. For example, what I regard as the distinctly unpleasant tom-cat smell of choisya leaves, others describe as 'pleasantly peppery', while the apparently heady scent of a bluebell wood in full flower completely passes me by. I have a friend who, when persuaded to stick his nose deep into a chalk-white, maroon-throated flower of the heavenly scented *Gladiolus murielae* (oops, I nearly forgot to include that one in this quick rundown) and breathe deeply, stares at me uncomprehendingly. Mind you, he swears blind that the foliage of *Melianthus major* smells strongly of peanut butter. Peanut butter? Ridiculous.

SULKY AGAPANTHUS

There has been much binding in my inbox of late on the subject of disappointing agapanthus. Well what did we expect, readers, after a tough winter?

The more common hardier hybrids that have become so popular, and of which there are now scores, have leaves that yellow and fade away for the winter. These are relatively hardy if tucked down into the ground in soil that is free draining – possibly less so if grown in pots outside and not given any protection or shelter in the winter. (Just as a tetchy aside: British gardeners seem generally slow to grasp that above ground can actually be a lot colder than below ground in winter here.)

The collective whinging has mainly been about those, generally known as *A. africanus,* that are slightly tender and rather more enormous and therefore much drooled and fussed-over. These behave a little differently and are just about evergreen during a 'normal' winter if moved, with considerable difficulty because they need to be in large containers, into somewhere 'frost free'. Typically *A. africanus* (including my own, so this is from a similarly suffering horse's mouth) have produced wonderful new leaves this year and absolutely no flowers. The reason is that our frost-free places were just not frost free enough last winter, it would seem. I have been giving mine its fortnightly water ration this summer laced with high-potash tomato food, even when it was clear that there would be no flower shoots forthcoming, in the hopes that this will boost it for next year.

Since my plant (a kindly donated offcut) has been in its pot barely three years and has been well treated during that time, I don't think that the lack of flowers indicates that re-potting is urgent and obligatory and I am hanging on to see what happens next year, resolving to be a bit more pro-active with frost protection in my unheated greenhouse if things turn nasty again. With gardening, hope springs eternal, after all.

DUSTY HONESTY

Earlier this summer a friend gave me some seeds that
she said were from her honesty plants (Lunaria annua).
Anyway, the seedlings have grown well in pots over the
summer, but yesterday I found them in a terrible state.
I have cut off 75 per cent of the leaves to try to save the
plants and in doing so showers of white dust rose up.
Is there any hope for them?
Gillian C, Bristol

White dusty patches on the undersides of the leaves are evidence of the fungal disease, white blister, to which honesty and other members of the brassica family quite commonly succumb. The fact that the seedlings of this biennial were stranded in pots a little longer than they should have been may have weakened them and made the problem somewhat inevitable, although overcrowded honesty seedlings growing in soil that is too dry will have been just as likely to suffer. Removing the worst of the leaves may just possibly help to save the seedlings, as will a drenching spray with a systemic fungicide such as FungusClear Ultra by Scotts once you have planted them out. If they survive, your seedlings will flower next May, though the plants may be rather un-magnificent. You can then save seeds from them and try again. Spores of the disease may linger in your soil, so you should always inspect the undersides of the leaves for early signs of it in the future, and even spray preventatively. 🌿

WINTER TUBS

Emailer Mary wants 'different' ideas for winter tubs. This same question came up at a Q & A session with some local Sussex luminaries. From Ed Ikin, head horticultural honcho at Nymans – pulmonarias. Jean Griffin of BBC Radio Kent and I both came up with a similar theme: evergreen plants that could later be transferred carefully to the garden. She chose the red-budded *Skimmia japonica* 'Rubella', and I plumped for icy-grey-leaved *Helleborus* 'Silver Dollar'.

PHLOX 'CHATTAHOOCHEE'

Please, what can I do to encourage my pot of Phlox *'Chattahoochee' to repeat its glorious spring performance next year? It seems happy in a rather small pot (roots are now appearing through the drainage hole), producing much new but worryingly brittle growth this year. And how do I*

propagate it? My inclination is always to leave things
alone, but I am learning that ruthlessness has its place
in a garden.
Sally, by email

I too absolutely love this little untidy little plant (*Phlox
divaricata* subsp. *laphamii* 'Chattahoochee' to give it its full
name), which has flowers of that particular shade of mauve-
blue that glows at dawn and at dusk (*Malva sylvestris* var.
mauritiana 'Primley Blue' is another...). Reluctant to grow
even more treasures in pots than I already do, I tend to plant
mine out in my rather cold/clay soil, and have to accept that
it is not at all robust. You are right, I think, to keep yours in
a pot, since this phlox (and the other little sprawly ones)
appreciates sharp drainage and tends to turn up its toes if
subjected to any kind of winter waterlogging. However (sorry,
a horses, bolting and stable doors thing), you should have
pruned it back to the bone just after it had flowered (in June,
therefore), to promote some sort of orderly and less brittle
new growth that would all flower next year. And now? If I
were you I would gently re-pot it (in loam-based compost) and
put it somewhere sheltered for the winter, since the exposed
roots and brittle stems you describe sound rather vulnerable.
Even though it is slightly late to do so, you should take some
cuttings of any bits that snap off during the re-potting process
as insurance. Trim a few of the straggliest shoots away in the
spring, and feed it as it starts to grow. 🌿

CONFUSED MAHONIA

Audrey's mahonia's horticultural clock is all at sixes and sevens. It has
flowered for the second time recently, having already done a pretty good
job late last winter. Normally she leaves it alone, towering as it does
above the back of the border, only cutting it back if it threatens to crowd
other shrubs. However, she is about to have her hedge trimming done,

and wonders if it would hurt it if, in the interests of economy and simplicity, she were to have it cut back now as well.

Un-pruned mahonias (of the thick-set, 'cartwheel', *Mahonia japonica* type) get extremely threadbare as they get old, particularly if they grow in the shade (which they happily will). This one sounds as though it could do with major surgery of some sort, by which I mean that the tallest and most gaunt stems should be cut right back. Generally there will be a small side shoot somewhere low down on each of the shrub's thick, woody stems, above which you can cleanly cut (revealing alarmingly bright ochre sap, incidentally). These shoots then grow rapidly and within a season or two will occupy the space previously taken by their leggy parent branches, before themselves eventually becoming gaunt and needing to be removed. This operation is generally done in spring, after the shrub's normal flowering time and just as it puts on its annual growth spurt. However, since Audrey's mahonia sounds from her description as if it is growing in a sheltered spot, it will come to no harm if it is cut back in the autumn. But it would be sensible not to feed the shrub at this point (as you would normally after pruning), to avoid the possibility of coaxing it into somewhat tender growth just before winter. Audrey should wait till next spring for that part of the operation. Whether or not – and indeed if it does, how much – this shrub flowers next spring after its strange flowering behaviour and off-season pruning is anybody's guess, I have to say.

SLOPPY LOPPERY

In strong winds my enormous shrub rose, an English Rose, took a bit of a bruising – its roots were nearly being pulled out of the ground. So I took my loppers and cut it down to about 2ft (60cm). Do I now just leave it or mulch it with manure? My husband is telling me to leave it, otherwise it will make too much growth now before the cold weather.
Helen, by email

It sounds also as though you need to tread the roots of the bush back into the ground (give it a good, slow drench first), since roses like to be tucked in really firmly. Follow this up with a comforting mulch around its base (your husband is right, this does not need to be rich and foody, since you are not expecting the rose to do much this late in the season – the remains of a bag of multi-purpose compost or home-made compost would be fine).

Apart from that, leave this rose well alone now until mid-spring, and then prune the branches again, down to an outward-facing 'eye' (dormant leaf bud) just a bit below the point at which you normally cut them in the summer, following this with mulch and feed. Roses are as tough as old boots – and yours should be fine, I think. 🌱

GROWING AN AVOCADO PLANT

I am sure this is not the first time you have been asked this, but I have grown a small avocado plant from a 'stone'. It is now about a year old. What do I do next, and what can I expect from it?
Graham, Middleton-on-Sea, West Sussex

A carefully sprouted avocado stone has the potential to make a handsome, large-leaved houseplant with a woody trunk, although it will most certainly not achieve its natural height – which is 20ft (6m) plus – nor will you get a crop of avocados.

Pot your plant on as it grows (I suggest you use a 50/50 mixture of multi-purpose compost and John Innes No 3). Keep it evenly moist (yellowing leaves will indicate that you are overdoing the watering), and give it a place in your home where it receives the maximum amount of sunlight. To encourage it to bush out and stop it becoming a single gangly stem, pinch out the growing tip (or prune it down by half if it has already become a bit leggy). Avocados can happily cope with a stint in the garden between June and September each year, but be mindful of rapidly proliferating leaf pests when you bring your plant indoors for the autumn and winter, and spray at the first sign of trouble with something systemic such as Baby Bio House Plant Insecticide (which may stop interlopers that might otherwise get the upper hand in a warm environment). ❧

HORSES, STABLE DOORS AND ALL THAT...

CL says that exceptionally mild, damp autumn weather played havoc with her overwintering plans, and she lost to botrytis (furry grey mould – see also July, page 87) a much fussed-over meconopsis that needs winter protection and that she clearly incarcerated in her greenhouse too early. You should have sprayed with a systemic fungicide before it went in there, CL, and eased off on the watering. And you should have just kept your eye on the thermometer and weather forecasts, and kept the greenhouse door wide open... Gardening is annoyingly full of the 'should haves' that optimists call learning curves.

HEDGE WOES

I have an ugly boundary hedge by the side of the steps leading to my front door, which I would like to replace. It is a few yards (metres) long, about 2½ft (75cm) wide and

5ft (1.5m) tall, sunny for much of the day in summer.
It is mainly elder (which smells awful) with self-sown
beech, sycamore, ivy. The brambles and a rose particularly
annoy the postman. With what should I replace this mess?
Ideally I would like flowers and/or fruit if possible.
Gwen, by email

I could, of course, write here what you want to read: a list of
half a dozen or so plants that would give you a wonderful
medley of colourful leaves, flowers and even berries: interesting,
low maintenance and postman-friendly all year round. But I
am not going to. The reason I am inclined to be somewhat
obtuse is that the area you describe is so narrow: I am having
trouble thinking of flowering shrubs suitable for a hedge that
would grow to 5ft (1.5m) in height that could be restricted to
such a narrow width. The larger hebes, escallonias, *Hypericum*
'Hidcote' and hardy fuchsias – all the usual flowering suspects –
would need to be cut back repeatedly at different times of year.
If they were simply treated as a hedge and shorn once or twice
a year they would look awful and not flower well at all.

So after much thought, I shall suggest something really
rather boring that you don't want to read, namely that you
would be better off planting a simple evergreen hedge, the
best of which is yew. At a pinch *Lonicera nitida* might do it,
as would somewhat boring privet. The other alternative, if the
area is really sunny enough, might be rosemary (the tall and
slim 'Miss Jessopp's Upright') that could be shorn just once
after flowering. If the whole idea sounds just what you didn't
want, then consider giving up the hedge idea altogether and,
subject to agreement with your neighbours (who would be
daft to disagree, I feel), putting up a small-squared trellis to
the desired height and growing a *Clematis montana* var.
wilsonii (the heavily scented one, my absolute favourite, worth
seeking out) on it. Plant it at the northern-most end of the
trellis, since it is bound to travel southwards. ❧

WHAT TO DO WITH WATSONIA

I have some Watsonia plants that have just finished
flowering. I'm not sure whether I should leave them in their
pots and bring them into the conservatory for the winter or
dig them up, let them dry off (in the conservatory) and
plant them out again next year.
Joan, by email

To a certain extent the answer depends on where you live.
Can you successfully leave your dahlias in the ground over
the winter? If you can, then you should be able to grow
Watsonias outdoors, since they need more or less the same
growing conditions – namely light and well-drained soil that
does not dry out in summer, in a really sunny sheltered site.

Watsonias (also known as bugle lilies) grow from corms
and are South African relations of irises and gladioli, some
varieties being hardier than others. It may be that you have
corms of the most commonly grown form, *Watsonia pillansii*.
In which case, if you live in the milder parts of the UK, i.e.
the southern or western counties, and can offer them a
suitable home outside, I would do so. You could either plant
them out now (planting them fairly deeply is a good idea)
and cover them with a deep, dry mulch for the winter. Or
you could dry off the corms and plant them in spring. If
they establish well, the corms may need dividing every
four or five years.

If on the other hand you can't provide them with
what they need, then keep them in their pots in a cool
conservatory, but keep the compost (which should be a loam-
based one, John Innes No 2) barely damp during the winter. ❧

140

COLLAPSING GRASSES

Several of my miscanthus and other tall grasses have been
knocked over by wind and rain. How can I stake them for
next year without the stakes being unsightly?
Barbara, Southend-on-Sea, Essex

The various forms of miscanthus make quite dense clumps
that all too easily get battered by winds unless grown in
amongst other more rigid tall perennials, which is perhaps
how they look best. These grasses are not evergreen, so can
(and should) be cut down in the autumn or winter. If grown
as specimens or in exposed sites, they do indeed need
supporting as they gain height. In the absence of a source
of tall twiggy sticks to use as virtually invisible 'props',
I use rusty metal structures because I find them extremely
unobtrusive. Where appropriate I put a single 5ft (1.5m) stake
behind the clump, and use a length of soft twine to encircle
it (quite high up), wrapping it around some of the individual
outer stems as I go. This is a bit of a fiddle, but the result is
inconspicuous, and the plant looks totally natural. 🌿

EVERGREEN SHRUBS FOR A WHITE GARDEN

My Surrey garden was planted by previous owners as a
'white garden' and I am keen to stick to this colour scheme.
I have bought some hellebores to plant in the area, which
is lightly shaded for part of the day in summer by a
neighbour's birch, but would like ideas for some evergreen
flowering shrubs that will grow to about 5ft (1.5m).
Melody, by email

The shrub that springs to mind if you want mid-summer
flowers is the white-flowered evergreen *Escallonia* 'Iveyi',
although with limited sun this might not flower so well.

141

There are a couple of other bland, colour-free evergreens that do a good screening job and will cope with light shade. *Elaeagnus × ebbingei*, which carries fairly insignificant white-ish flowers in very early autumn that smell heavenly – like lily of the valley – has new summer leaves that are an eye-catching silvery-bronze. *Viburnum tinus* might also be a good choice – flowering in spring and again in late summer if you are lucky. The variety 'French White' has buds and flowers that are dead white instead of pink-ish. These shrubs could be clothed, once established, with summer-flowering clematis such as white-flowered viticella clematis 'Alba Luxurians' or large-flowered C. 'Huldine' if you gave them a bit of TLC to get them going.

But do you have to have flowers? The following have evergreen-and-white leaves: *Pittosporum tenuifolium* 'Silver Queen' or *Rhamnus alaternus* 'Argenteovariegata' (Italian buckthorn). They would both associate very well with your hellebores, I think, and could brighten the light gloom at the back of your garden, too. 🌿

WHEN SHOULD YOU MOVE A CLEMATIS?

Harry from Lancashire asks when is the 'right' time to relocate an established clematis. The answer is that the only *safe* time is during the months when it is dormant. Late-flowering clematis (group 3) are in some ways the easiest to move, since when you cut them down from their supports – which you have to do in order to do the deed – they re-grow the following spring in their new home and should flower that same year. Early flowerers (groups 1 and 2) will not flower the spring after being cut back in winter, but should flower well the following year. Inevitably some root damage will occur when you move any clematis, since the root system on an established plant will be extensive, having supported all that top growth. (See July, page 83, for details on how to plant to give it the very best chance.)

THINGS TO CONSIDER IN OCTOBER

❋ This is the best time to order bare-rooted hedge plants. Prepare a wide trench incorporating organic matter and bonemeal into the soil. Plant them 12–18in (30–45cm) apart in a staggered row.

❋ When planting out young wallflowers, make sure their roots are well down in the soil and be sure to firm them into the ground.

❋ Sow some sweet peas in Rootrainers (that encourage the formation of strong, healthy roots) now.

Must do before winter
❋ Bag up last year's half-rotted leaves so that you don't put new ones on top of old.

❋ Cut back ivy and other climbers from gutters and protect downpipes from falling leaves.

❋ Check that tree ties and supports will withstand storms.

❋ Remove some of the heavy top growth of big bush roses in exposed sites to prevent wind rock.

Garden tidy up
❋ Late-flowering clematis that are really unsightly and have no redeeming attractive fluffy seed heads can be reduced now by half (then properly cut right back in spring).

❋ Spray roses that were badly affected by blackspot and mildew in late summer and clear up fallen leaves to stop spores lingering.

Good housekeeping
❋ Clean out greenhouses. Wash out old summer flower pots and plant saucers. Wash bird feeders and scrub bird tables.

143

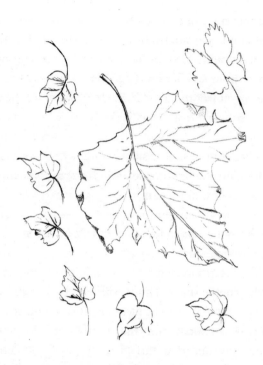

November

LIFE UNDER OAKS

Every November my front garden briefly becomes a source of extreme horticultural angst. Surrounded by tall evergreen hedges, the thin patch of lawn becomes obliterated for days under the mass of sopping leaves that hail down from an enormous overhanging oak. I know that when all the leaves are down, the unrelenting rain stops and the ground dries so I can get out there, order will be restored. But the particularly dismal situation this month brought to mind a reader wanting low-maintenance ideas for a similar site to mine where not much thrives. I decided to look on the bright side and give some guidance, citing my own efforts as proof that there is indeed life under oaks.

Hard though it is to imagine now, various parts of my currently sparse little lawn break out in spring to reveal rashes of snowdrops, aconites and other spring-y thingies that do well under deciduous trees. The grass perks up after a feed, I start mowing it and it stays reasonably green for most of the year despite the shade. This is partly down to a generous amount of moss – this is not a place to be picky about sward quality. Close to the oak trunk there is a natural colony of the easiest of native ferns, *Dryopteris filix-mas* (the only one that thrives in summer-dry soil), as well as spreading mats of white-flowered ground-smothering sweet woodruff (*Galium odoratum*), *Geranium macrorrhizum* and the evergreen *Euphorbia amygdaloides* var. *robbiae*, whose acid lime-green 'flowers' illuminate the gathering gloom as the oak leafs up. Still well under the oak's canopy, I have planted some shade-tolerant and good-looking shrubs, some evergreen, some deciduous. Leaf contrasts are all important and flowers are few, although martagon lilies thrive and white-flowered honesty (*Lunaria annua* var. *albiflora*) and foxgloves self-seed here and there. Under and around the shrubs clusters of cyclamen flower in autumn and early winter, following on with wide rosettes of beautifully marked foliage. An urn containing a big stripy hosta is a focal point, and I also heave large pots of pale lilies into strategic positions in summer.

It all works – but not without considerable initial effort. Giving up so much sun and sky to the oak tree has huge drawbacks, not the least of which is the annual cascade of fallen leaves. I am, effectively, gardening in a wood, so it is important to make the most of this resource that otherwise just gets trapped in drifts, choking the undercarriage of garden hedges. By blowing them into piles (with an ultra-light battery-powered leaf blower from Bosch) and chopping them up with the mower before composting them in huge wire cages hidden behind the shrubs, I use the resulting leaf mould to improve my root-y, neutral/slightly acid soil, mixing it with a little bonemeal before planting and also using it each spring to mulch heavily around the newer shrubs as well as a pair of original rhododendrons. After at least two seasons of careful nurturing to get them established (i.e. clawing back the mulch to deeply drench their roots once or twice in high summer before replacing it), my newcomers are, several years on, growing well. While November is not and will never be anything other than frustrating, the little area has earned itself a grand, if somewhat ironic name: 'The Leaf Garden'. The dappled light out there is particularly enchanting on hot mid-summer afternoons. Remember them?

Shrubs that cope with my root-y neutral-ish soil and dappled shade: *Leycesteria formosa, Viburnum plicatum* f. *tomentosum* 'Mariesii', *Hydrangea quercifolia, H. macrophylla* 'Madame Emile Mouillère', *H.m.* 'Merveille Sanguine', variegated Portugal laurel (*Prunus lusitanica* 'Variegata'), *Hoheria* 'Borde Hill', *Abelia* × *grandiflora, Cotoneaster lacteus, Corokia* × *virgata* 'Bronze King', *Pittosporum tenuifolium* 'Tom Thumb', *P.t.* 'Irene Paterson', *Daphne odora* 'Aureomarginata'.

AUTUMN COLOUR

Where can I buy a maple called, I think, 'Red Sunset'? I visited relations in New England in the 'fall' and this is the name of one of the trees that particularly caught my eye amongst several with superb and long-lasting autumn colour.
Edgar, by email

Various tree specialists will be able to help you with this. I see that Barcham trees (barcham.co.uk), for example, have several varieties of *Acer rubrum* on their list, of which 'Red Sunset' is indeed one of the best for autumn colour.

And now for the slightly depressing bit. Autumns in North America are, I understand, both protracted and glorious not simply because of the species that grow there (although as with the ornamental Japanese maples we love to grow in our gardens for their colour, the big acers that you saw turn a particularly good colour because the glucose trapped in their dying leaves happens to turn bright red). The basic climate has a huge part to play as well, with consistently long hot summers that give way suddenly, rapidly to cold winters, which we simply do not have. We do have many wonderful trees, including our native oaks of course, that colour up and give a spectacular show, but alas not every year. And it strikes me that even with the right kind of leaves, we all too often have the wrong kind of autumn. But don't let my Eeyore-ishness put you off. Go and find your 'Red Sunset', and enjoy whatever it gives you as a reminder of your trip. ❧

CLIMBER REPLACEMENT

In view of my advancing years I am gradually removing things that require a lot of time and effort pruning. To replace my rampant Akebia quinata *on a south-facing house wall, I am considering planting two strongly self-*

supporting roses that will complement each other and grow
to a maximum height of about 6ft (1.8m). I don't like red,
pink or yellow, and they must be very disease resistant –
unlike, for instance, 'Händel'.
Dene, Hythe, Hampshire

You have put me in a bit of a straitjacket with your colour
limitations, but as far as all the rest goes – height, disease
resistance, the need to be self-supporting and so on – there
is no question about it. In my opinion, Rugosa roses are
absolutely the best choice: *R. rugosa* 'Alba' is a white, single-
flowered variety that might suit you. The roses themselves
are heavily scented and, as a bonus, bright orange-red hips
the size of cherry tomatoes follow the flowers.

   The way these robust roses grow is an absolute gift to
gardeners of advancing years – well, Dene, let's not beat about
the bush, you said it. Apart from the very few glamorous
double-flowered varieties (you should steer clear of the double
white 'Blanche Double de Coubert', for example) that are
grafted on to the rootstock of wild roses, and that don't,
incidentally, reliably produce good hips anyway, Rugosas
spread out over time by producing suckers that flower in their
second year. Thus two planted side by side would meld into
one within two or three years. There are varieties that will
grow to 6ft (1.8m) or more, and once they are established,
height can be pretty well controlled with annual early spring
pruning: the very oldest shoots, and any that are growing
where they shouldn't, can simply be cut out at ground level,
middle-aged ones halved (or their heights staggered), and
the stoutest of the young ones left un-pruned to push on
upwards. Anything that gets too tall can be lopped or
vigorously deadheaded in mid-season, and will simply
shoot out again. Rugosas don't seem to be at all attractive
to greenfly, nor do they get mildew or black spot, and their
leaves turn a fabulous bright buttery yellow in late autumn. 🌿

RAINING ACORNS

Our two tall oaks have produced an absolutely massive crop of acorns – the biggest for 20 years or so. I spent an hour yesterday (enjoyably in the sun) picking up acorns from a large flowerbed and the adjacent lawn. Am I going to spend next year digging out young oak trees?
Jane, by email

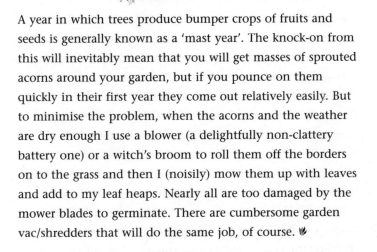

A year in which trees produce bumper crops of fruits and seeds is generally known as a 'mast year'. The knock-on from this will inevitably mean that you will get masses of sprouted acorns around your garden, but if you pounce on them quickly in their first year they come out relatively easily. But to minimise the problem, when the acorns and the weather are dry enough I use a blower (a delightfully non-clattery battery one) or a witch's broom to roll them off the borders on to the grass and then I (noisily) mow them up with leaves and add to my leaf heaps. Nearly all are too damaged by the mower blades to germinate. There are cumbersome garden vac/shredders that will do the same job, of course. ❦

TREE STAKES

I have been told that a rowan would be a suitable tree to plant in the rough grass at the end of my garden, since the site is slightly exposed to the wind after the removal of my neighbour's large conifers. Should I go ahead, what is the best way to stake it?
Malcolm, by email

It's all in the tree's other common name, mountain ash: yes, a rowan is a pretty safe bet for a draughty site.

It is now generally accepted that if trees are left to their own devices, as they are in natural woodland, and allowed to wave around a little in the wind they will form stronger trunks more quickly. However, in an even moderately windy site, solitary and exposed garden trees are best given a short stake, about 30in (75cm) above ground, 24in (60cm) below, angled so that it leans about 45 degrees into the prevailing wind, fastened with a strong, rubber, buckled tie. This is particularly necessary with pot-grown trees, which take a few seasons to anchor themselves to the surrounding ground and are therefore more vulnerable. Another favoured but slightly more obtrusive-looking way of supporting trees is to use two straight stakes, one each side of the trunk, placed so that the prevailing wind doesn't shove it towards either, and tied with a buckled tie of equal tension to each.

However you stake your trees, they will not need support for ever, and as they grow in those first years you should check that the ties and buckles are in good fettle and loosen them as necessary. One further tip (relevant perhaps since this tree is to be planted in an area of 'rough grass' that may presumably be strimmed on occasion): buy an extra tree stake and bang some 16in (40cm) long, sawn-up sections of it into the grass around the trunk of the tree (avoiding its roots, obviously). This is an excellent way to prevent future bark-strimming incidents, which can prove fatal to young trees. ❧

ACANTHUS – ALL LEAF, NO FLOWERS

Peter is losing patience with a three-year-old acanthus that refuses to flower. In my experience acanthus can take an age to settle down and I think Peter should put away his spade for one more year at least, and apply some sulphate of potash around the plant next spring to coax it into floral action. It is also my experience that if you give up and try to dig acanthus out, you always leave a bit behind which, thus hacked about, sulks even more.

RESCUING A 'BURIED' HYDRANGEA

Philip and his wife have found a beautiful but threadbare hydrangea 'buried' in the back of beyond in their new overgrown garden. How can they rescue/move it? They have nothing to lose if they cut 90 per cent of it down, leaving untouched, if feasible, any new young green shoots that are coming from its base. Carefully digging it out and replanting it in good leafy soil elsewhere, there is every chance it will shoot anew next spring. But it almost certainly won't flower until the following year. Fingers crossed.

COMPOST NOW AND AGAIN

I have a smallish garden and a 140 litre (5 cu ft) compost maker. It takes most of the year to make reasonable compost and it is ready now. When is the best time to distribute it – now or in the spring?
Geoff, by email

You are not the first reader to ask this question, which becomes somewhat pressing at this time of year when a single bin like yours may be full of ready-to-go compost from last year's garden output and space is needed in which to compost everything from this year's clear-up. The long-term solution to this problem is to try to find space to tuck away a second bin, or even a third, which will obviously alleviate the pressure considerably.

The answer to your question, however, slightly depends on what you want to do with your compost – whether you simply want to use it as a surface mulch around existing plants to protect them or conserve moisture, or to improve the soil more generally further down by using it when you plant, adding it (with Rootgrow or a little slow-acting bonemeal) to the soil that you tuck back around bare roots and soil balls. If you want to use it as a mulch, then it is best if you bag it up now and keep it under cover until spring. It will simply go on rotting down and therefore, if anything, improve in quality.

Personally, however, I find that since home-made compost is never perfect, it is best used as a soil-improver in a different way, by incorporating it into the soil under newcomers at time of planting, so that any rogue seeds that have evaded the composting process will not pop up everywhere. So if you have some planting still to do, use your compost now. 🌿

COMPOSTING CARNIVORE POO?

Kathryn asks if she can compost badger dung. While the poo of rabbits and guinea pigs (herbivores) are excellent compost bin additions, in theory badger poo is not ideal, since badgers are in fact (like dogs and cats) carnivores – their favourite grub being worms and large insects. However, should Kathryn add a smattering of badger poo to the contents of an otherwise well-balanced bin, I doubt if the world will stop turning.

COLCHICUMS

The flowers of my pink autumn crocus have now died down. Is this the right time of year to move them?
Margaret, by email

It is best not to disturb autumn crocus corms when they are in active growth, or you risk upsetting them so that they will not flower the following year. The time to do the job if you must is in high summer, around July, once the leaves have died down completely. Re-plant them in informal groups, about 3–4in (8–10cm) deep.

Finding a suitable site for colchicums can be a bit

problematic. They look rather fetching flowering in the naturally dry-ish soil at the base of trees and large shrubs, but this sort of place may not in fact be a sunny enough site in the spring/summer to encourage a lot of autumn flowers. 🌿

A TOADSTOOL TANTRUM

A comforting word or two for P D, who says his 'garden is full of toadstools at the moment'. He (or indeed she – it can be a bit embarrassing when readers don't make this clear) asks if they will harm plants and what should be done about them. The vast majority of toadstools are harmless to plants, and are all part and parcel of the essential biology and general organic rot that goes on out there in the soil, most of it completely unseen by gardeners. The toadstools that should ring alarm bells are those of honey fungus – orange capped, each with a distinct collar around its stem, generally thrown up in clusters from underground roots or cut-down stumps of their host plants in the summer. If rashes of autumn toadstools annoy, they can simply be swept away with a broom.

MONTBRETIA MENACE

I have tried really hard to get rid of a mass of what I am told is montbretia that has not flowered at all in the three years I have lived here. I pull at it in the autumn – bringing up quite a lot of corms attached to the dying leaves, and fork around the soil to pick up others, but every spring the boring leaves come back with a vengeance.
Valerie, by email

Although rather lovely when it 'escapes' from gardens and grows informally on the wrong side of the fence, montbretia (*Crocosmia × crocosmiiflora*) stops flowering when overcrowded, and congested clumps are hard to get rid of. Like you, many gardeners want to be shot of this thuggy thing, particularly now it has been upstaged in recent years by its far more interesting and less invasive relations.

As you are finding, the more you try to heave out the clump, particularly by clutching at the stems that snap away from the corms so easily, the worse the problem gets. Where you are managing to winkle out single corms with their foliage, what remains in the ground beneath each, namely, a previously attached 'stack' of old corms from earlier years, will produce little, and any under-sized corms (the result of all the years of congestion) that break away in the mayhem won't be productive either.

What you need to do is fork around much more deeply, loosening the soil in the whole area and removing entire stacks, intact if possible, as well as any detached young ones. Inevitably you will miss some, so don't be tempted to plant anything new in the seemingly bare patch of soil you have created – particularly not one of the smarter new crocosmia varieties, or things could get very confused – until mid-spring. Then you will see just how much you missed and have another go with your fork to get out the stragglers. On no account put the discarded corms in your compost heap or they will haunt you, invariably flower-less, for ever more. ❦

ASSET STRIPPING

My plant of Rosa moyesii *'Geranium' had its hips stripped by blackbirds as early as September. I seem to remember that some of the suppliers of this rose state that it carries its hips all winter. Is my experience common?*
Patrick, Co. Antrim

For once we can't blame the fertile imagination of the writers of purple prose in plant catalogues for the failure of plants to live up to expectations. I suspect that this is just a symptom of the weather extremes that decimate gardens. Hedgerow fruit such as blackberries and hawthorn suffer too, which means that the birds have been quicker than usual to snap up what was available to them in our gardens. The hips of this glorious rose are spectacularly visible, so no wonder they were snaffled so early. It is certainly disappointing, but should act as a reminder as to how hard winter can be for birds, and how important we and our gardens are to them. ❧

KAMIKAZE WORMS

My husband has a black compost bin that gives us good results. When we remove the lid to add more material there are dozens of small worms writhing around the edge as though trying to escape. Is this normal? It is difficult to replace the lid without damaging livestock.
Helen, by email

These writhing worms are brandling worms that do much of the creative composting in your husband's bin (and in wormeries, see also April, page 28. Quite distinct from familiar earthworms, in nature they like snuggling down in deep damp leaf litter and need constant moisture in which to do their work in the bin. They naturally gravitate upwards just before it rains to save themselves from flooding, I understand. (How they know it is about to rain is beyond me, so 'pass' on that one.) There is not a lot you can do apart from flipping as many of them as possible back into the bowels of the bin. Incidentally, I do like the idea of the compost bin belonging exclusively to your husband. Perhaps you could ask him to do the worm-flipping if you find it distasteful. ❧

TOUGH TALK

Chris from Cornwall sent me a picture of an ailing dracaena, well over ten years old, wide, lofty and branching, that has until now flowered wonderfully every year. This year it flowered and immediately started to drop its 'fronds', and now looks decidedly unsightly. I have a theory about these tender aliens that seem to cope with our climate, even though they are not really supposed to. They are fine for a few years while they are small enough to be sheltered by other plants, but once they become tall enough to be affected by cold winds and frost their life may be cut suddenly short. If their roots survive, they will produce numerous half-hearted sprouty bits but never regain their former majesty. Not what you want to read, Chris, but this plant has had its day. Off with its head. And, while you are at it, of course, out with its roots.

THINGS TO CONSIDER IN NOVEMBER

❋ Late-flowering shrubs that are an eyesore (e.g. *Buddleja davidii*) can be cut down by half and returned to in late February for a proper job.

❋ Lollipop potted bay trees are vulnerable to frost. Drag them under the eaves if possible, bubble-wrapping their trunks at the very least.

❋ Keep un-netted garden ponds as leaf free as possible, fishing out debris daily if necessary.

❋ Rotary mowers inevitably become seriously clogged with mud in autumn. Clean them each time to avoid having to chip away at an undercarriage thick with rock-hard clods next spring.

In the flower borders
❋ There is no great rush for the autumn clear-up, and certainly don't work on your borders from a saturated, worm-cast-covered lawn. Wait for the ground to dry and then seize the moment.

156

❀ When cutting down new and unfamiliar perennials, leave 6in (15cm) stumps to remind you where they are.

❀ Drag pots of lilies, which are perfectly hardy, under the eaves or somewhere where they won't stand in puddles.

❀ Bundle the tatty stems of ornamental grasses together and tie them up with twine before cutting them down, to save a lot of bother clearing up afterwards. One-handed Jakoti shears speed up this job.

❀ Tulips and other spring bulbs should all be planted out by the end of the month.

Tending to tender stuff

❀ Dahlias grown in big pots are caviar for vine weevil grubs. De-pot, inspect, dry off and keep tubers somewhere frost free for the winter if you suspect vine weevils are at work in your garden.

❀ In colder gardens, protect tender precious perennials (cannas, dahlias) in the ground with dry mulches (e.g. bracken under pegged-down fleece) rather than bubble wrap or polythene.

❀ *And finally…* Pick the last of your roses and bring them indoors, even if they are not perfect, to enjoy a last whiff of the glorious summer. And when the weather is vile and you are sick of the sight of your garden, sit in your socks with your feet up and rifle through the new seed and plant catalogues.

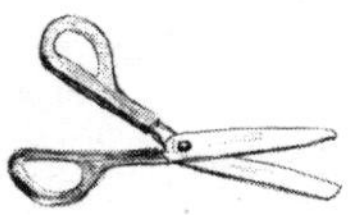

Winter

December

WINTER STRUCTURE

December is the month when I receive frequent letters from mournful readers complaining that their gardens have become dreary, with far too much of the required 'structure' being provided by last year's grasses and seed heads, which are all now looking forlorn. Can I suggest, I am asked, evergreens to plant that will cheer things up? So for the benefit of who knows how many of you (but I bet it's a lot), I'll have a go here.

There is no doubt that winter gardens cry out for plants that are evergreen, and this generally, but not exclusively, means shrubs. The skill is planting enough to create some structure and leaf/stem shape/colour contrasts, preferably (as experts love to tell us) using plants that are also interesting at some other time of year via flowers/berries or colourful spring leaves. To be avoided are shrubs that are all a bit same-y. A cherry laurel/rhododendron/*Prunus lusitanica*/*Viburnum tinus* overload (one that I have had to pare down and dress up in my garden) smacks too much, frankly, of a dank Edwardian shrubbery, despite various floral contributions in spring. A limited use of the odd bit of variegation is useful, although some gardeners can't stand it, I know.

Top of the list of winter-value shrubs must go *Daphne odora* 'Aureomarginata' (minimal variegation here, but there are February flowers with stunning scent). And while on the subject of winter/spring scent, I have to slot in *Sarcococca hookeriana*, magnificently tolerant of deep shade and, for large gardens, the 'cartwheel' mahonias (such as 'Lionel Fortescue'). Other leafy favourites of mine are *Olearia ilicifolia* (pale, matt, holly-style leaves); *Pittosporum tenuifolium* 'Silver Queen' (tall, variegated), 'Irene Paterson' (smaller, marbled variegation) or 'Tom Thumb' (dwarf, dark red leaves, lime-green spring shoots); *Brachyglottis monroi* (small, crimpy grey foliage) and *Phlomis chrysophylla* (woolly grey leaves that turn olive-bronze in autumn).

In my garden the tiny dusky-dull leaves of *Corokia* × *virgata* 'Bronze King' cheer up a boring laurel backdrop immensely. Stems are important

161

too: in winter, those of another corokia (deciduous *C. cotoneaster*) resemble stark, black, tangled wire-netting – great in early winter with sedums and grasses. Deciduous *Cornus alba* 'Elegantissima' dresses its ruby-red winter stems with cream-variegated foliage in summer. But the green-leaved varieties have possibly even better winter stems: *Cornus sericea* 'Flaviramea' has golden stems, while those of *C. sanguinea* 'Midwinter Fire' need no further description.

Finally, although I'm generally only asked about shrubs, I feel compelled (as I look out of my window for inspiration) to tack on a few other plants that earn their keep during the winter. Self-seeding in my mild garden I am lucky to have leafy evergreen herbaceous *Geranium palmatum*. Its foliage may yet get a bit of a battering if we have snow, but it looks great right now. Elsewhere, the silver-grey foliage of perennial stock could almost be described as 'architectural'. Amid the bronzy foliage of *Libertia* 'Taupo Blaze' I can see last summer's flower stems now laden with dull-orange berries (that birds seem to shun), while close by (as an unexpected bonus) the maroon-leaved, non-invasive tall perennial *Persicaria* 'Red Dragon, that dropped its leaves in late October, now has scarlet arching stems that will persist till January. The shoot tips of a mature *Euphorbia characias* subsp. *wulfenii* are curled over like shepherd's crooks, ready to produce huge heads of other-worldly lime-green bracts in a few weeks' time. Snowdrops are up, there are catkins lengthening on the hazel and littered here, there and, oh heavens, seemingly everywhere, the new growth of various pulmonarias is already swollen with flower buds. Take heart. Next month, spring, we hope, will be just around the corner.

SCENT-SIBLE ADVICE

I suppose it was to be expected: my enthusiastic piece about a clutch of useful evergreens to both brighten winter gardens and tickle the olfactory senses resulted in a flurry of emails from gardeners experiencing problems relating to three of them.

First in line is Sheila from Hampshire, who has been growing *Daphne odora* 'Aureomarginata' in her garden for the past three years, expecting delicious February scent. She is still waiting. Her daughter, who lives nearby, has a ten-year-old specimen that is equally shy to flower. Both shrubs receive a few hours of sun a day (is that just in summer, I wonder?), and are planted in chalk soil that is improved with compost. Somehow I don't think it is about the chalky (limey) soil: daphnes are not as fussy about soil pH as you might imagine. It could be a lack of direct sun from autumn to spring: plants grown in sunnier (but not blisteringly sunny, parched) sites seem to flower rather better than those growing in winter gloom. It could also be that they are being fed too much by their anxious owners, particularly with nitrogen-rich fertilisers that tend to encourage lush foliage at the expense of flowers. If these were my daphnes, I would be meaner to them – just give them sulphate of potash (which encourages the production of flowers) twice a year, in spring and late summer/early autumn.

Janet feels cheated, never having noticed any scent from her pittosporum. I find their sweet, lily of the valley scent is most noticeable in the evening, on plants grown against sunny walls. Flowers are produced in early summer; they are tiny, colourless and tucked in amongst the leaves, and are followed by little nut-like seeds.

Another famously strongly scented spring shrub, sarcococca, is continuing to disappoint Jill in Lamberhurst. Once grown unsuccessfully in a pot and now even more unsuccessfully in a prime sunny spot in the ground, she can't decide what to do with it next. Sarcococcas are serious candidates for areas of poor soil and deep shade, so if I were Jill I would dig it up in the next few weeks and move it to somewhere rather more horrid (it is not a good-looker for most of the year anyway, and she can replace it with something considerably more fun-in-the-sun). My own patch of sarcococca grows alongside a scruffy path between garage and back door, so at least I catch its deep-winter scent as I pass. Flowering on the previous year's growth, sarcococcas benefit from a trim in late spring. In Jill's case that will mean the removal of about 4in (10cm) of growth that should have flowered – but didn't.

GEORGE AND FREDDIE ARE VERY SORRY...

George and his son Freddie are getting into deep, deep trouble with Her Outdoors. They are wondering if there are any football-proof shrubs that would make good Very-Sorry-and-Happy-Christmas presents. Hang your heads in shame, lads. Try getting her *Olearia macrodonta* and *Brachyglottis* 'Sunshine', and fervently hope that big evergreens hit the spot and melt her heart.

'ANNABELLE' IN A MESS

I was hoping that the papery, brown, dry old flower heads of my young and beautiful Hydrangea 'Annabelle' *would remain as a lovely feature in my garden through the winter, but after awful weather most of them have become unattractively battered. Will the plant suffer if I cut them off?*
Susan, by email

Unlike the mop-heads with which we are more familiar, this beautiful, refined and very hardy hydrangea flowers on new growth each summer – in fact, the harder it is pruned in spring, the bigger and better its flowers will be. I understand why you are asking the question: in all but the warmest gardens the old flowers of more tender mop-heads are traditionally kept intact throughout the winter and until the danger of sudden frost and icy wind has passed. They do provide some sort of protection for the pairs of vulnerable flower buds, already plumping up for next summer, to be found a little way down each stem. But do go ahead and remove the tatty flowers of your 'Annabelle' since they look such a mess. You can even prune it hard now if you want, cutting it back to a low-ish framework on which buds will appear and from which everything will shoot next spring. Or if it suits you better, you can do it in March. 🌿

164

DECEMBER DAFFODILS?

Something for Penny to note: the name of the daffodil that she was stunned to see flowering outside in December is *Narcissus* 'Rijnveld's Early Sensation'. Bulbs are fairly widely available (but not at this time of year, obviously). I got mine from Avon Bulbs (avonbulbs.co.uk).

UNDER PRESSURE

Does my husband really 'need' a pressure washer for Christmas, so he can keep our small paved area, which does tend to go green with algae every autumn, pristine?
Anonymous, Plymouth

Clearly battle lines have been drawn here and you are hoping I will stand on your side. Well, I will.

For cleaning mud off the car, hosing down the dog (I'm joking…) and generally having noisy, water-wasteful fun – maybe. Pressure-washing is a man thing, as we all know. But for the removal of a bit of green algae on a patch of paving? The job can be done with far less hullabaloo, using a stiff broom, a bucket and a suitable plant-friendly cleaner such as Algae & Mould Stain Cleaner by Biotal. Mind you, it will probably be you that ends up doing the job, since men who hanker after power washers don't do humble broom-ing.

However, if it absolutely has to be a serious Christmas toy, could you not try to steer him off in another direction? How about a nice quiet, environmentally so-much-friendlier garden shredder? ❧

165

CIRCULATION PROBLEMS

My wife says she read somewhere that you should always take pumps out of ponds in the winter. I maintain that constantly circulating water in our small pond will help to stop it from freezing over and endangering fish and other pondlife trapped beneath. Could you umpire for us?
Greg, by email

All things considered, it is probably sensible to take the pump out. This gives you an opportunity to clean it properly, and also gives the mechanism a rest. In my experience pond pumps have a 'life', and have a nasty tendency to conk out, like car exhaust pipes, just after they come out of guarantee. Furthermore – and this depends of course on the size of your pond and how things are set up – in prolonged cold snaps the circulation pipes can freeze solid and force the pump to shut down, which is generally not a good thing. Float a hollowed-out piece of polystyrene packaging on the pond surface to maintain a patch of unfrozen water. ❧

A BIT ABOUT BIRDS

Although poor old wood pigeons and herons get a pretty universal thumbs-down from gardeners, many of you are I know pretty passionate about other more benign garden birds and indeed feed them and provide water for them all year round (as we are encouraged to do).

We have been warned in the past by the RSPB not to put out nuts in plastic mesh nets since the netting presents a hazard to birds. We are encouraged instead to transfer the contents to proper feeders. These soon earn their keep by enabling us to buy seed and nut supplies in bulk, which saves a fortune and solves the peanut/net problem in one fell swoop. What about all the netted fat balls on the market, though? I give my local friends fat and seed-filled coconut half-shells at Christmas instead of giving them cards. The shells can of course be endlessly refilled using lard (which is the best fat for conditioning feathers, according to the RSPB) as a base for a seedy, nutty or oaty 'cake' of some sort, which blue tits in particular absolutely love.

Flying in the face of polite opposition from RSPB experts, who have in the past told me that my very simple bird food 'recipe' for ground feeders – oats moistened with just enough vegetable oil to make them weather and wind proof – was not in fact ideal, I am mentioning it again here as requested by readers. Animal fat goes rock hard, so it would not work for my ground feeders: blackbirds, dunnocks, wagtails and even shy thrushes, who seem to relish it. It would also render it irresistible to rats, I suspect. And feedback from readers who picked up the oat/oil tip from me a few years back tell me they supplement it with bits of chopped apple, etc, and are rewarded with masses of happy birds in their gardens all winter long.

POST-LUNCH OVER-ENTHUSIASM

Words of comfort for Bill, whose brother-in-law went 'a bit berserk with the hedge trimmer' after a 'festive' lunch before Christmas, rendering a rather saggy mature lonicera hedge 'almost bald' on one side. Will it recover? Yes, but it will take some time – maybe a year. Bill should look on the bright side – this drastic treatment will actually benefit the saggy hedge in the long run. He could maybe plan a similar festive lunch next year and let his gung-ho brother-in-law loose on the other side.

COMPOST BINS... NO NEED TO PANIC...

Emailer Margaret's compost bins are usually well populated with brandling worms (the little wriggly red ones) which always appear as if by magic (see also November, page 155). This winter they have vanished completely and show no sign of returning. She asks if she should buy in a new population of them.

The answer is no. The brandling worms will have gone to ground, that is, hunkered down, become extremely inactive and stopped breeding because of the extreme cold. They should snap into action again and will reappear, as Margaret puts it, as if by magic, when the weather and the contents of the bins warm up a bit. Meanwhile, there are other beneficial forces at work in the compost bin anyway – woodlice, millipedes, bacteria, moulds, slugs and so on, so there really is no need to worry.

Mrs R is having a bit of a compost panic of a different kind: she was mortified to find some uninvited and extremely unwelcome guests – namely a couple of vine weevil grubs – in the first spadeful of compost that she extracted from her bin. She assumes she will have to get rid of the entire contents. Well, personally I wouldn't: I strongly suspect that these grubs are in there because she disposed of the contents (compost and all) of an infested little pot of dead something-or-other recently. There is, after all, no reason on earth why adult vine weevils would have laid their eggs in the bin in summer – they always choose places where their grubs will be able to survive by eating fresh young plant roots. Furthermore, once disturbed, grubs don't survive. She could simply make herself feel a bit better about things by going through the top few inches of compost to check for any more interlopers and, as I usually suggest, feed any she finds to the robins.

PRUNING JAPANESE ACERS

I have a couple of Japanese acers in large pots so that they can be moved to an area sheltered from the bitter east wind. Unfortunately, they have grown lopsided and rather too large for the space available. I seem to recall that it is difficult to prune them without damaging them or worse, and would appreciate your advice.
Clive, by email

You can prune these maples sparingly, but you should do it now, since the sap of maples rises very early in the year and they have a tendency to 'bleed' if cut in late spring or early summer. By all means go over the trees in the growing season and remove cleanly any dead wood – bleached-white-looking – which is particularly susceptible to coral spot rot, a fungal disease, if it is left hanging around. This is one of the very few fungal diseases that can attack living plant tissue.

Also next year, when the tree is in leaf, assess the overall shape again (so important with these elegant trees) and even earmark branches that should be shortened the following autumn by tying coloured string around them. I would get into the habit of occasionally turning the pots during the growing season, which may stop them growing quite so lopsided. 🌿

RE-POTTING AND ROOT-PRUNING BOX TOPIARY

I have two spiral-shaped Buxus sempervirens *that are now just over 4ft (1.2m) tall, in lead containers that are 18in (45cm) wide. Both of them seem to be suffering. I would like to re-pot them in the same containers, adding fresh compost. I have read that you can reduce the size of the root ball by cutting it down vertically. Is this practical and, if so, when should it be done?*
Rachel, by email

Re-potting any shrubs of this size is something that can largely be avoided if you initially plant them in containers that will give the plant enough root space to accommodate its growth to the eventual size you want it to be. This may sound a bit obvious, but it is surprisingly commonplace to see large specimens suffering in the equivalent of tight shoes: in pots where there is not even room to feed the plant and water can barely penetrate the compacted root ball. However, if you get

169

things right from the start and the container is large enough, you can for many years keep its occupant happy simply by annually replacing the top few inches of compost within it, incorporating slow-release or other balanced fertiliser granules as you do so.

You don't mention their depth, but your containers would seem to be on the borderline as far as the size of your box spirals is concerned. If you have never tried the compost replacement trick, you could perhaps give it a go. Box is remarkably greedy and needs feeding twice a year (in spring and in mid-summer after clipping), and it may be that your plants are just a bit starved.

Re-potting and root-pruning is the other option. Do it now: cut down vertically to remove up to 30 per cent of the total root ball of each of your box plants. Since the containers are so heavy, it may be easier to cut them in situ, using an old breadknife or not-your-best pruning saw, before carefully removing the much-reduced plant and clearing out what remains from the pot before re-planting. New compost should be John Innes No 3 with a little coarse organic matter added. ❧

GROWING MISTLETOE

Sarah wonders if she can use the berries from the mistletoe she bought to grow some of her own on an old apple tree. Would that this were simple to do, but it isn't – particularly if Sarah has had her mistletoe hanging for a long time in a heated house, so that the white juicy berries have shrivelled and dried up. If she can get hold of mistletoe berries in good condition at the right time, however (February or March), or if her mistletoe is still in good condition and she can preserve it by keeping the stems in water somewhere cool, she could painstakingly 'plant' seeds in the crevices of her old tree (a job normally done by the birds, particularly mistle thrushes, that love to eat them). For those who are determined and have a lot of patience – once germinated, the seeds take several years to produce mature plants – there is a small illustrated booklet that will help explain the process: *Grow Your Own Mistletoe* by Nick Wheeldon (available from mistle.co.uk).

WOOLLY APHIDS

For the past three years my 14-year-old pyracantha,
growing against the house wall, has become increasingly
infested with woolly aphids. I have sprayed with a hose
and then with a systemic insecticide but to no avail.
Am I on a losing wicket?
Brenda, by email

I am afraid you may well be. Woolly aphids that commonly infest trees in the apple (*Malus*) family as well as pyracantha and cotoneaster are the very devil to defeat. These super-aphids have worked out a way to survive: covering themselves en masse in a protective grey-ish woolly coating (that is often mistaken for a fungus of some kind) to keep predators at bay – and that includes us and our spray bottles of gunk, of course – and breeding like billy-oh every spring. Infestations caught early on small plants can be shifted and dealt with: the waxy-woolly protection can be stroked away with methylated spirits or even shifted with a gloved hand, making the insects vulnerable to insecticides, or whole branches can be simply scrubbed with a brush dipped in soapy water. However, this is not really practical where your huge and prickly pyracantha is concerned.

171

The best you can do is to prune the whole plant back hard after it has flowered next spring, sacrificing next year's berries completely. You will be pruning out the worst of the breeding colonies, and should clear up every scrap of debris afterwards and burn it. Then feed the roots with a general fertiliser (they will be extensive on such a mature shrub), water it in and apply a thick mulch of organic matter. Maybe then you can do some scrubbing, hosing, etc and spray the new growth when it appears with Provado Ultimate Bug Killer Ready to Use. This may mean that the following year things look a little better, and it will flower on any healthy new growth. But I doubt if you will see the problem off completely. 🌿

BAMBOO INVASION

Out of control invasive bamboo seems to be a worse (and harder to tackle) plague than the Russian vine epidemic of the 1980s. Back then, the rampant climber, so beguiling when espied on holiday, draping its froth of white flowers over a crumbling French cowshed, for example, was planted without a thought throughout the suburbs with the aim of hiding eyesores and obliterating neighbours as quickly as possible. Fortunately it is now seldom seen on sale, and gardeners appear to have learnt their lesson – I often see it scrambling out of control over railway embankments, but seldom where it can really offend.

So bamboos are the new garden bogeymen – possibly, I am sorry to say, with the encouragement of all those garden makeover television programmes. They became for a while the fast-green-screen material of choice for numerous overlooked gardeners, and now perhaps a subsequent generation of house-owners is paying the price. While some varieties are clump forming and more or less behave themselves, others such as the unknown variety now sending up viciously vigorous spikes in emailer Ann's lawn (after her valiant attempt to dig it out of a border), are capable of travelling many yards via stout underground rhizomes, boring their way through membranes and landscape fabrics into the bargain.

The advice generally given about getting get rid of bamboo involves using a determined combination of digging (as Ann has done) to get out the main core of the plant and use of the strongest forms of glyphosate available to gardeners. These include Roundup Ultra 3000, Bayer Tough Rootkill, Bayer Super Strength Glyphosate or Doff Knockdown Maxi Strength Weedkiller.

Tall bamboos that can neither be tackled with a spade nor sprayed should be cut down in winter and the new growth sprayed in the spring while it is still of manageable proportions, but you will almost certainly have to apply even these strong weedkillers more than once. Where rhizomes have got into a lawn, as in Ann's garden, the job of weedkilling is doubly horrendous, and a certain amount of collateral damage is to be expected.

The 'safest' hardy, clump-forming bamboos (that are therefore happy long-term in large containers) belong to the genus *Fargesia*: *F. murielae* is attractively 'weepy', *F. nitida* is more upright. Taller bamboos that eventually form much looser clumps but are not regarded as badly invasive if grown in the ground are to be found in the genus *Phyllostachys*. There is a lovely one with stems that turn golden with age, and another whose stems turn shiny black. They can both be grown in containers for a few years, but may then run out of steam.

Bamboos look best if they are regularly 'groomed', and the oldest stems cut out to make room for the new ones. Black and golden stems look more dramatic if their lower side shoots are cleanly removed. Bamboos in containers whose leaves go 'tubular' are telling you they are short of water.

THINGS TO CONSIDER IN DECEMBER

If the weather is mild
❋ Snails will have gone into hibernation, but look for opportunist slugs, and treat them with various pellets or SlugClear by Scotts (a liquid).

❋ Even this late it is worth taking cuttings of argyranthemums (marguerites), which may still be green and flourishing in the absence of frost. They are less prone to botrytis than other soft-stemmed plants and will slowly root if they are kept barely moist in a frost-free greenhouse.

❋ Outside, finish cutting back perennials. Once the borders are cleared it is a good time to winkle out colonies of hairy bittercress and the spreading runners of creeping buttercup.

❋ Open the greenhouse door to allow the air to circulate during mild days, but don't forget to close it at night.

❋ Lanky new shoots of rambling roses growing on fences and pergolas should be tied down, not cut off. They will carry the best of next summer's flowers.

❋ Carry on pruning and tying in climbing roses (aim to finish by Christmas), cutting back short shoots that have borne flowers to within a couple of dormant buds (leaf scars) of their main 'framework' branches. (If you're not sure of the difference between climbing and rambling roses, see page 180.)

Clean and tidy
❋ Check that evergreen shrubs in wet soil have not been half pulled out of the ground by strong winds. Haul them upright, provide a stout support or two if necessary (tree stakes/ties or Flexi-Tie) and tread their roots very gently back into the ground.

❋ Untidy, un-pruned lavender (ideally it should have been done in August) will look better if you just shear off the old flower shoots. Harder pruning will be due in February.

❋ Clean out and renovate old nesting boxes. Birds need a long time to get used to new boxes which, incidentally, make excellent Christmas presents for friends as do other bits of garden bird paraphernalia.

January

GETTING DOWN TO IT AGAIN

Except in truly vile weather, I manage to keep to my morning routine. You know the one: out there first thing, an old fleece slung over crumpled jimjams, steaming breakfast cup in hand, reviewing the whole place inch by inch, tweaking and making plans. However, motivation understandably wears thin in deepest winter, and while timing is crucial for a few gardening jobs, it's not for all. Seldom is it possible to do things by the book anyway; most of us just dash out in winter and do what we can, when we can, and it all has to be a matter of common sense – the understanding of 'why' and the mastery of 'how' being just as important as the timing. I confess happily, therefore, I seldom do what I advise you readers to do and if I do, rarely do I do it when I advise you to do it.

So now that particular cat is out of the bag, let's have a bit of a play with it. Faced with a depressingly scruffy garden that has had very little done to it since the end of the summer, and with short days that are likely to be either wet or frosty, what are my own priorities? What in the way of cosmetic surgery is really urgent?

Key job no. 1: the vine growing against the wall near my work room – I look at it every day and so I can't ignore it – got the text-book treatment straightaway while it is definitely dormant, new growth being cut off to within two buds of the main framework of branches and put through the shredder.

Pruning my climbing roses was another priority. As with the vine, shoots were cut back to within two buds of the main stems and any strong new shoots oh-so-gently (so they didn't snap) tied in to the main framework.

I actually found that leaving massive herbaceous clumps such as *Persicaria amplexicaulis* until they had all but collapsed before cutting them back made them easier to compress for composting, as was the saggy foliage of hollyhocks, sweet cicely (*Myrrhis odorata*) and lady's mantle (*Alchemilla mollis*). I found myself still being quite selective, however: another persicaria, 'Red Dragon', has several luminous red stems that still look good, so it will not go under the shears until it gets ugly; nor will the mahogany brown seed heads of bog irises and rodgersias, the beige whorls of *Phlomis russeliana*, or anything else that is relatively good-looking and upright, for that matter.

A shady stepping-stone path in the lawn had become muddy and mossy in winter, partly because an admirably shade-tolerant but rather thuggish geranium flops over it in summer and the grass thins out. I attacked the geranium with a spade to curb its spread and then cut some pliable hazel stems from my allotment hedge to bend into low hoops to make a miniature fence each side of the path. The little fence cost nothing, looks rather pretty and will just do the trick next summer. I will re-seed the grass between the stones in April. N.B. By the time this idea found its way into this book, I had decided to replace the wooden hoops with lovely curved iron ones (from Leander Plant Supports, leanderplantsupports.co.uk). Lower maintenance. Money well spent. Very smart. You see, readers, nothing is written in tablets of stone.

Once all the cut greenery had been binned or shredded-and-binned, my inner housewife took over and I simply went on a tidying spree. It seemed quite batty when I was doing it, but I edged the lawn with shears and very gingerly plastic-raked the turf clear of debris, noticing that a rash of crocus leaves were up already. Finally as I swept the paths and paving with a stiff brush I realised that me and my garden were re-bonding for yet another year.

MONEY PLANTS

I took a lovely matching pair of money plants out into the garden during a mild spell in the autumn and then forgot about them. Being a distinctly fair-weather town gardener, I did not venture out for a few weeks over Christmas. Imagine my horror to discover them recently – one has turned rather black, the other has some signs of life. How can I revive them?
Jana, by email

More crimes are committed against houseplants in winter than most of us have had hot dinners. Too often they are wilfully abandoned somewhere out of sight, out of doors (dinner-party hydrangeas in particular suffer this fate, see March, page 12). Others are killed with kindness when they should be drying off and having a resting period. Instead they die a lingering death ankle-deep in saucers of foetid water.

The money plant – crassula – is a tolerant, succulent plant and will put up with incredibly low light levels and out and out neglect, including no water. Which is why it has become a firm favourite with indoor stylists, completely 'non' gardeners or 'fair-weather town gardeners', such as you.

The plant that has gone black has undoubtedly had it. The other one may just possibly revive if you bring it indoors to a cool, light room, cut it back to the lowest signs of life and let its compost dry out completely. My guess is that you will have to replace them both. ❦

HOW TO LOOK AFTER SEASONAL HOUSEPLANTS

While we're on the subject, here's how to look after various houseplants properly.

Christmas cactus needs a resting period in early spring, when it should be kept dry at the roots and cool. In the summer the pot can go outside for the stems to ripen. In September return the pot indoors to a cool room with no artificial light. From late autumn give it a warmer, lighter site and a fortnightly liquid feed. Don't move the pot around, and avoid temperature fluctuations and over/underwatering – or developing buds may start to drop before they open.

Flowering 'houseplant' azaleas will flourish indoors in the short term only, if kept in cool rooms and regularly watered with room-temperature rain water. Although their botanical clocks are awry because they have been forced into flower early, they will eventually adjust if planted outdoors in suitably acid soil (or pH neutral soil plumped up with ericaceous compost or leaf mould), preferably in dappled shade.

Potted cyclamen are sold to us by the squillion in early winter. But after a very short time in the dry atmosphere of centrally heated houses they go downhill. Misleading sloppy labelling such as: 'Excellent in patio containers and hanging baskets. Flowering time late summer onwards. Suitable for full sun or partial shade. Deadhead to prolong flowering,' makes me see red. These pretty little flowering cyclamen (I believe they are hybrids of *C. persicum*) will indeed flower through exceptionally mild winters outside in containers in sheltered urban southern courtyards. They look like the real thing – UK-tolerant outdoor *C. coum* and *C. hederifolium* – but hardy they ain't. My advice on caring for them? You can't – give up.

ROSES: RENOVATING CLIMBERS AND RAMBLERS

I am frequently asked to explain how you can tell whether your 'climbing' roses are true climbers or ramblers. A quick tip, for the truly foxed: if your 'climbing rose' flowers once, around late June/early July, and then produces masses of barely controllable new growth, it is a rambler (and will flower best the following year on however much of that new growth you train and tie in, having removed some of its oldest, exhausted growth where feasible). If your rose flowers from June and goes on flowering a bit until the frosts, on short shoots that emanate from a woody, quite gnarled framework, and furthermore doesn't make much in the way of new growth each year, it is a climber. Climbers need annual pruning in winter and flower the following year on yet more short shoots produced the following spring. Ramblers grown on structures are incredibly high maintenance, and are best if allowed to leg it up trees, where they can be left to, well, ramble. Lower-maintenance, more controllable climbers are better suited for training against walls, arches and fences, but do need occasional major surgery. There is, of course, more to it than that, but answers to the following questions that pinged into my inbox recently may be enlightening.

Kate's 'American Pillar' rose has been climbing over an ornamental metal structure for the past 30 years or so. She has cut back some of the older shoots by half, a few times after flowering, but the whole tangly, towering edifice has become completely top heavy and has now fallen over. To get the metal structure upright she needs to be brutal with the rose. Just how brutal can she be? Very, is the short answer. 'American Pillar' is a rambler of immense vigour – I have grown several in my time and know it well. Each year such roses produce long pliable shoots from the ground or from their lower halves, and early each winter I used to deconstruct my roses, cutting the older growth down to the ground and winding the new shoots around large purpose-built rustic chestnut pyramids, making sure that some of the shoots clothed the lower parts of each structure so that they would be more or less covered in blooms when they flowered. In high summer they would produce a mass of pale-eyed sugar pink flowers from stout laterals growing from the wound-around framework – a fantastic sight for about four weeks. So... to completely renovate her roses, Kate can cut all the older shoots right back and just preserve one or two – or as many as is practical – of the youngest, to wind around her newly straightened support. These should produce some flowering laterals this coming summer and can then be cut to the ground next winter. Properly fed and mulched this spring, the rose should subsequently produce numerous new shoots that can be wound around the support as they grow and tied in properly next winter to produce a fantastic show the following summer.

David's 'Climbing Iceberg' rose problem is slightly different. Although there are wires on the 6ft (1.8m) wall against which it grows, little of the rose is actually attached to them, and he would dearly like to cut the rose down and do things properly, training and tying in the new growth more or less horizontally to improve its looks and flowering potential. Can he cut the rose hard back, he asks? Yes he can, but since this is a climber, it will not make such a quick recovery as Kate's rambler, and he will certainly not get a lot from the rose for a couple of years while it re-creates the necessary woody, more or less permanent framework from which climbers flower. It would be better, perhaps, if David were to take things slowly: saw out one or maybe two of the oldest and woodiest parts of his climber now, either to the ground, or to just above a point from which newer, greener shoots are evident. These comparative youngsters may still be pliable enough to pull gently downwards and tie to the wires. If he then trims off the shoots that bore flowers last season (they probably still have hips on), down to a couple of leaf scars (the site of dormant buds) from where these emanate, the scar/buds will grow into new short growths that will flower next summer. Furthermore, the removal of very old shoots (and subsequent feeding and mulching of the plant) will certainly have encouraged it to produce one or two new ones – most probably from near to the ground. These can be bent and eased gently into roughly horizontal positions and tied to the wires as they grow next summer, and will form strong replacements for yet more of the old, untrained growth that David can saw out next winter. This way, the rose should more or less renew itself over two years.

COLD COMFORT FOR REAL BEGINNERS

When an exceptional freeze-up starts early in winter and goes on and on in a Canadian sort of way, we all start to get a bit nervous: so what must real gardening newcomers make of it all – readers such as the one who wrote to me alarmed that her hostas had disappeared? Here are one or two in-a-nutshell winter basics. Bear with me, those with loftier and more detailed know-how.

Deciduous shrubs (weigelas, etc) caught by an early frost before they had a proper 'autumn' will remain festooned in crisp browning foliage.

They are not dead and will gradually shrug off their old leaves and leaf up again in spring.

Common or garden herbaceous plants (as sold year-round from open-air areas of nurseries – phlox and so on) are frost hardy. Most die down in the winter (as with any 'rules', there are exceptions) and the majority, like the reader's hostas, disappear without trace and re-emerge in spring.

'Perennials' sold only in summer (often from polytunnels, along with annual bedding plants) – pretty lantanas, fancy shrubby fuchsias and such – definitely need frost-free winter protection if they are to go from year to year. Any that were left outside can therefore (along with the inhabitants of summer containers) be regarded as dead. Finally, when the ground is very cold, we should expect a late spring-growth kick-off.

AND SNOW'S NO FUN EITHER

Several readers are wondering about the long-term effects of a thick, lingering blanket of snow on their gardens. The good news is that some of the worst leaf-damaging pests may take a hammering and will be less troublesome next year (although after a pretty icy winter, capsid bugs still went on the rampage in my garden in summer). Be aware, however, that snails hibernate and slugs just dig themselves into the soil, to re-emerge as soon as there is a whiff of spring in the air, so we shouldn't get too excited. While thick snow acts as an insulating blanket, frosty winds do much more damage, mainly to the exposed shoot tips of evergreens from slightly warmer climates. Pragmatism is helpful: we should expect some damage to our cistuses, ceanothus, and so on. Whether or not to knock snow off evergreens that are bent double under the weight of it (thereby exposing the vulnerable shoot tips) is a perplexing question. You have to use your own judgement based on the original habitat of individual plants. I find most branches that are bent double tend miraculously to bounce back, so it pays to leave them covered and carry out first-aid pruning later. Waterlogged soil, once the thaw sets in, is potentially more damaging to our plants, I suspect.

TIDYING UP FERNS

I don't normally do anything about the ferns, some evergreen and some not, that grow at the side of a path in our rather wild woodland garden, where things are more or less allowed to do as they please, but this year I notice they are looking particularly messy. Will I do them any harm by cutting them all right back?
R F, by email

Most of the ferns we grow, such as the ubiquitous *Dryopteris filix-mas*, are deciduous. Depending on the weather, they tend to completely collapse by November, fresh fronds starting to curl upwards in early spring. By all means cut them back: I have just taken the shears to my own fern wreckage and put the remains on my leaf heap. They can of course be cut back earlier and used as a useful insulation layer under pegged-down horticultural fleece, to provide protection for various tender plants.

Evergreen ferns, such as our native hart's tongue, are normally treated rather differently. It is usually sufficient to go over them in early autumn, tidying them up so that they provide a bit of welcome smart structure to a winter woodland garden. Snipping out the oldest and tattiest leaves makes a big difference, and may even make them produce a few bright new fronds before winter kicks in properly. Growth then starts again in earnest as spring arrives. If you have never 'groomed' your ferns in the past, they will come to no harm if you do a total renovation job on them by cutting them right back now.

The sooner the better, in fact, so that you don't run the risk of damaging the all-new and beautiful crop of fronds that will start to form shortly. ❦

INVADERS

Barbara from Leeds seems remarkably unfazed by the rat that has made its home in her compost bin, and asks if she can leave it there until the spring and if she does, will it contaminate her compost. The answer is no, not really – but the rat will probably continue to cause a certain amount of local upheaval. However, as long as Barbara is only putting garden greenery and other dross, together with vegetable and paper-based domestic waste (not meat, fish, eggs or cheese or anything tainted therewith), it will just be using the place as a temporary warm lodging. Personally, I think I would upend everything, evict Monsieur Rat, and put a couple of layers of tough wire mesh underneath the bin before replacing the compost.

Moles, moles and more moles... they seem to be invading James' Oxfordshire garden. Should he use the molehill soil as potting compost? Yes, a lot of gardeners do, because it is fine textured and virtually weed-seed free. Mixed with equal quantities of sieved leaf mould and fine sand, it makes a rather good seed-sowing medium, in fact. However, when I was similarly plagued by our velvet-coated friends, I used to just brush the molehill soil around with a besom. Or I would scoop it up and store it in bins, mix it 50/50 with sand, and put it back from whence it came – using it as lawn top dressing and, if anything, concentrating its application where I could feel softness in the lawn where the moles had tunnelled.

CLIMBER FOR A NORTH-FACING WALL

Emailer Letty has a gap on a north-facing wall of her bungalow that she feels is suitable for a climber, preferably one that is evergreen or semi-evergreen, and asks for ideas. Well, of course, I could trot out a short list (and it is rather short) of climbers that would do the business tolerably well without the benefit of direct sun: *Hydrangea anomala* subsp. *petiolaris*, various decorative ivies, Virginia creeper (parthenocissus), one or two roses (including 'Albéric Barbier' and 'Mermaid'), and so on. But bungalow walls being squat, I am inclined to suggest that a climber would be a bit of a handful, getting into gutters and roof tiles in no time at all, eventually involving a lot of tussling from the top of a ladder (as I have to do with the climbers planted by my predecessor on the shady side of my garage).

Instead I suggest Letty looks at wall shrubs that are tolerant of shade. How about *Garrya elliptica* with its green February tassels, Japanese quince (*Chaenomeles japonica*), even a mahonia, whose architectural cartwheels of prickly foliage and scented winter flowers face determinedly outwards towards the light? Maintenance would, of course, involve annual pruning, but fixing small-gauge trellis firmly to the wall before the shrubs are planted would make it easy to tie in branches as they grow.

BLIND BULBS

My husband and I moved into a house that has a high, 40ft (12m) long (quite sunny) hawthorn hedge. Last year we were delighted to see a row of daffodil shoots growing along its length. Unfortunately, none produced flower buds. In an attempt to coax them into flower, we cut the hedge down to 8ft (2.4m) and thinned out and fed the daffodil bulbs with slow-release fertiliser. The leaves are appearing again – do you think they will flower? And if they don't should we dig them up and plant new ones?
Claudia, by email

It may depend on how many years the bulbs were starved and overshadowed, or should that be 'blinded', by the hedge, which, when it came into leaf, denser and taller each year, starved the daffs of vital sunlight just after they flowered – precisely the time that they needed it to enable the formation of the next year's buds within their bulbs. They could have been in that state for many years: alive, leafy – but increasingly unproductive.

After all the trouble you have taken, it would be churlish of me to suggest that you are on a hiding to nothing with these bulbs, but I have to say I have never managed to re-vitalise blind bulbs. Actually, I'm fibbing: I have gone to great lengths, and during my first spring in my current garden I did a meticulous trowel-prowl, winkling out all the (scores of) blind daffodils I could find. If I were you I would give your rogues this one chance, and if they don't behave properly after all your TLC, then heave them out and replace them. You may have to dig down very deeply indeed to get them out if they have been there for many years, and whatever you do, don't resort to simply removing their leaves through sheer frustration or you will get in a real pickle. Also, be aware that if the hedge thickens up and is allowed to creep upwards again, any new bulbs will inevitably go the same way as the old ones. So perhaps it would be a good idea to plant replacements further away from it. ❦

THINGS TO CONSIDER IN JANUARY

Stay indoors if it's vile

❋ Order snowdrops to be delivered 'in the green' in a few weeks' time and peruse the new seed and summer bulb catalogues.

❋ Use up the remains of last year's liquid tomato feed (high in potash) by fortnightly feeding indoor flowering plants.

❋ Re-pot any lilies that have been in the same container for three years or more (in finger-numbing weather this may be a messy kitchen-table job). Use John Innes No 3, with 20 per cent added leaf mould (or multi-purpose compost).

❋ Don't overwater citrus bushes. Let them dry out between occasional drenches laced with a winter citrus fertiliser.

❋ Really bored? Clean hand tools, and wipe secateur blades and pruning saws carefully with WD40.

Get outdoors if it isn't

❋ Prune established Rugosa roses, cutting close to ground level the very oldest shoots and the skinniest shoots, and halving the remainder.

❋ Get new container-grown roses into the ground now, if the weather is mild enough.

❋ Spring bulbs may be popping up all over the place. Those in grass that are likely to be crunched underfoot can be protected with hooped barriers made from hazel.

❋ Cut back the last ornamental skeletons of winter – seed heads of agapanthus and *Iris sibirica*, for example. Take care with the stems of big border sedums lest you damage the new shoots.

❀ Snip away now the straggly remains of the perennial, shade-tolerant lime-green spring dazzler, Bowles's golden grass (*Milium effusum* 'Aureum').

❀ In the unlikely event that the ground is dry and there is no frost (it does happen sometimes), you could mow the lawn on a high setting. This tidies up the garden no end.

❀ But don't be too tidy: leave some debris in scruffy corners as shelter for garden wildlife.

February

FOUR STAGES OF GARDENING

As I see it, the phases in an increasingly obsessive amateur gardener's life go something like this:

1. The shopping phase. Plants are salivated over, magazine-gardens hankered after, car boots are filled, receipts hidden. Too many plants are shoehorned in and moved about on an almost weekly basis. Deaths are frequent. Pests cause minor palpitations. A sense of panic creeps in with the ground elder. Why does nothing grow?

2. The over-nurturing phase. After a hectic year or two, something has to give. Plants that survive are likely to be overfed and fussed over, but gradually better understood. Books are acquired, other people's gardens are visited and gardening courses attended: received words of wisdom are adhered to rigidly. This phase can last for several years as a garden starts to settle, but two key factors – pruning confidence and weedling/ seedling and plant identification – gradually change the look of the whole garden.

3. About five years into a garden's life, with a fair wind the whole thing calms down. There is far less impulse-buying, although a good plant fair (from which we never come home completely empty-handed) and a one-to-one with an enthusiastic nurseryperson are still the horticultural obsessive's equivalent of a couple of stiff pre-prandials or a good night out at the theatre. Compost-making techniques are nailed, propagation becomes a serious issue and 'special' plants are exchanged between friends. The garden has a longer season, and all-or-nothing areas are either rare or deliberate. Self-seeders are properly appreciated; colonies of spring lovelies are at last allowed to fill out here and there where they will, so that gradually a garden acquires a natural-looking permanent 'ground floor' – something that probably looks, to stage 1 and 2 gardeners, somewhat out of control. But this is real gardening. You now confidently 'do your own thing' and while you feel that visible bindweed marks you out as prematurely past it, you give up on all but the worst infestations of ground elder. These are truly the golden years for both garden and gardener.

4. With increasingly stiffening limbs, unless you have help or find the energy to move to something smaller, your beloved garden, around which you still totter daily with great delight, gradually gets away from you. But that's fine. You can't see/don't notice the growing chaos anyway.

I am thoroughly enjoying a protracted stage 3. How are you getting on?

WHEN IS 'DEAD', DEAD?

Diana's *Ceanothus* 'Pershore Zanzibar' and Ted's *Pittosporum eugenioides* 'Variegatum' have both suffered appallingly this winter. The leaves of Diana's shrub have 'all turned brown', while those of Ted's are dropping off 'by the shedful'. Can either of them expect miraculous recovery?

I have to say that the outlook does not look particularly good. Even green-leaved versions of these shrubs are not especially hardy in the UK and are likely to suffer during hard winters unless grown against walls or otherwise well sheltered: ceanothus is, after all, a native of the warmer parts of North and Central America, while pittosporums come from Asia and Australasia. In both cases the variegated cultivars are even less hardy than green-leaved ones, and *P. eugenioides*, possibly the most elegant of the variegated pittosporums, is pretty notorious for giving up when the going gets tough. I even lost one of these in a not-particularly-hard winter in my mild London garden – in my view it should be sold with a health warning.

Once the leaves of a ceanothus – or any evergreen shrub for that matter – have all gone completely brown, there is little hope of it reviving (Christine from Lincolnshire, this is for you, and also Jane and her thoroughly browned-off variegated hebe). You can scrape the bark with your nail (if it is green, there is life) and adopt a 'wait and see' policy, living with the wreck until early summer and – if you are extremely lucky – some new growth will appear lower down each branch. After a hefty prune, the shrub may survive. If the shrubs in question are elderly, and the frost has caused the bark around the base to start splitting, however, there is not much hope of recovery.

Shocking, sudden leaf drop, such as Ted's shrub is going through, might be less serious, but only slightly. Ted will also have to wait, and prune his shrub back later in the season (he has done it once before, and it did come back), but things may never be quite the same again.

SEASIDE HEDGING PLANTS

Gilly wants ideas for a seaside hedge in Budleigh Salterton, Devon. She has grubbed out the Rugosa roses (what a shame), is now thinking of escallonia, but asks if I have any other evergreen ideas. Ubiquitous tamarix, of course, or how about *Atriplex halimus* (silver-leaved and only semi-evergreen, but very salt-wind tolerant, I am told by a friend in Cornwall, who grows it with great success and loves it). Read on for more seaside planting.

PRIVACY FOR A SEASIDE BALCONY

I am looking for a shrub for an east- and sea-facing tub on a balcony on the first floor. It receives sun to 1pm in high summer and less in winter. It needs to grow quickly (to be a screen between the adjoining balcony), to be evergreen, thrive on neglect and intermittent watering in the normally benign climate of the Isle of Wight. Is there such a plant or am I asking for the impossible? At the moment I have, as recommended by an Isle of Wight nursery, a Muehlenbeckia complexa. *It has never thrived but just kept its head above water and we give it another chance each year.*
Jenny, by email

I am presuming that you have put a trellis between you and the next-door balcony, since you mention having tried growing the rather weird and wonderful *Muehlenbeckia* (like coarse, twining horsehair, with distinctly minimalist foliage).

Your previous adviser was looking in the right direction, I feel: towards New Zealand plants, some of which have thick, leathery leaves and are known for their wind/salt tolerance. I think I would move away from climbers, however, and look at evergreen shrubs, training/pruning/tying them on to the trellis. How about olearias (*O. macrodonta* is the toughest), senecios (now brachyglottis) and some of the thicker-leaved hebes? Admittedly these shrubs could be viewed as slightly 'boring', but with the site you describe you are really up against it and I don't think you can afford to be picky – and if privacy is what you are after, you couldn't do better, really. You may have to put up with some leaf-loss (or worse) if we get exceptional frosts – it is just a fact of life in the UK in such an exposed site. Regular late spring or summer pruning will mean that you don't get much flower from them, but evergreens, as I seem to say rather a lot, do form an excellent backdrop for pots of temporary summer colour of some sort. 🌾

TRANSFORMATION FOR AN UNWANTED POND

My daughter and family are moving to a Thirties semi with a good-sized garden that has a circular brick-built raised pond about 8ft (2.5m) across. She has two children under two and for safety reasons she would like to get rid of the water. Have you any suggestions for planting up the brick structure, since it would be costly and time-consuming to remove it?
Lesley, by email

Rather than giving up on the wet stuff altogether, your daughter and her husband have an excellent opportunity here to create a small bog garden – an area of permanently moist soil in which can be grown some wonderful moisture-loving flowering plants. The job should not be too arduous since the pond liner is already there – it just needs modifying.

There is no 'good' time to disturb all the water wildlife that will inevitably be lurking in the sludge at the bottom of the pond, but I would suggest carrying out the work in early autumn. The pond water should be siphoned off on to the garden and the sludge scooped out (much of the livestock in it will miraculously find itself somewhere else to go). The pond liner should be punctured once or twice per square yard, so that it will drain, but very slowly, with something sharp (a Y-stake or a garden fork). Then add a 3in (7.5cm) layer of gravel and a similarly deep layer of garden compost, before filling the pond with a well-mixed blend of equal amounts of leaf mould (or ericaceous compost), fine-ish grit and loam-based John Innes No 3. Ordinary garden soil should not be used because it will inevitably contain weed and other seeds.

Once filled, the area should be watered until the surface is wet. The soil level will sink as it very slowly drains, and should be topped up before a selection of wonderful things is planted in it: various bog primulas, *Iris sibirica*, colourful sedges, rodgersia, *Caltha palustris* (king cups), mimulus and so on. Thugs such as wild yellow irises or a stripy spreading grass, *Phalaris arundinacea* var. *picta* (gardener's garters), should be avoided. A good local aquatics shop should have a selection, and as always there is a book that will help: *The Rock & Water Garden Expert* by Dr D G Hessayon (Expert Books).

To help with watering, it may be a good idea to install perforated hose around the edge of the area, invisible apart from the connector to which you attach the supply hose. Since the centre will be hard to reach, it may be helpful to put a large visually attractive rock or other inanimate object there. Plants should spread and naturally self-seed, and apart from ensuring even moisture, annual work will involve cutting back the old flowers and foliage in the autumn. ❦

CLIMBERS AND DEAD TREES

The fondness of gardeners for growing climbers up old and especially completely dead trees is quite understandable when you think about it. What could be more natural? After all, our wonderful old bluebell-carpeted woodlands are littered with glorious entanglements of native honeysuckle, wild roses and ivy, either clambering aloft or slumped artfully over mossy old stumps. Why should we not hanker after the same 'look' in our gardens?

Emailers Lee and Tom want to grow roses over a 12ft (3.6m) tall branching stump of an apple tree, central in their garden, and want to know if they should 'treat' the stump beforehand, while Ion from Norfolk has set his sights on smothering a dead monkey-puzzle tree with something glorious, to form a dramatic backdrop to his duck pond.

I really should advise these readers to go into things with their eyes open, however. Firstly, they should try to ascertain why these trees died because, to highlight a worst-scenario problem, they might be harbouring honey fungus. Rashes of mid-summer orange toadstools around the base of the stumps or (growing off their roots) in the area several feet away might indicate this. Old stumps can act as hosts to this fungus, which can travel via underground rhizomorphs to any susceptible or vulnerable living trees and shrubs nearby and kill them. Privet hedges are notorious for being the first local casualties. Gardeners are always advised, therefore, that it is 'best practice' to remove dead trees and as much of their roots as is possible, rather than make a feature of them.

Even if there is no sign of honey fungus, and gardeners decide to adopt the familiar 'oh, what the hell, life is too short...' attitude, growing climbers up dead trees is still not without medium-term complications. The roots of the stump or tree will naturally rot away anyway – you can't 'treat' them to prolong their life. The added weight of a great mass of rose or clematis will cause dead branches to snap prematurely, and make toppling of the whole glorious caboodle in a high wind far more likely. And then there is bound to be some general maintenance, all that wobbling around on ladders... Oh, this is just too depressing. I bet Lee and Tom and Ion all go ahead and do what they want to do anyway. I probably would.

RENOVATING POTS OF LILIES

Juliet, a self-confessed fair-weather gardener, has had some lilies (variety unspecified) in a pot in her London garden and they have come up smiling for several years without any particular input from her, she says. This winter the pot has cracked badly and is falling to bits. Something clearly has to be done as a matter of urgency. Is this the year she has to get her hands muddy before the weather warms up, she asks?

Indeed it is – and Juliet should get on with the job without delay. The lily bulbs, hopefully plump and healthy, should be carefully tipped out of their broken home. They may already have produced stubby new shoots and quite a lot of root, and should on no account be allowed to sit around and dry out during this operation. Three or four bulbs will sit happily in a new, heavy pot about 12in (30cm) high and wide, and when re-housed they should end up in the middle of the pot, with as much compost above as beneath them. Gutsy loam-based John Innes No 3 is always recommended for permanent planting of perennials, bulbs and shrubs, but it does have a tendency to dry to a rock-hard crust, so the addition of a little home-made compost or leaf mould (or, if not available, some commercial bagged multi-purpose compost) is a good idea, in order to loosen up its texture a little.

Although Juliet seems to have got away without doing anything in the way of annual maintenance with these lilies, I have to say that it is generally advisable to scrape out the top 3in (7.5cm) of soil each spring and replace it with a fresh layer of the mixture described above and a little slow-release fertiliser. Every third or fourth year, they should be completely re-potted while they are dormant – around January.

I have to admit that I also do a little bit of stealthy and incredibly careful investigation with my index finger in lily pots at around this time of year to make sure everything is as it should be. One year I took their perennial toughness for granted, only to find that all my pots had been infested with vine weevils and that the grubs had demolished the lot. For me, summer isn't summer without the scent of masses of potted lilies, so now I buy a few new ones each year, just to be on the safe side.

PLANTIFYING A BORING PATIO

I have a large uninspiring north-facing patio (flags on a hoggin base). The cement grouting having disintegrated, I would like to grow small plants in the cracks (having been inspired by the south-facing terrace at Hinton Ampner in Hampshire). What would be the best growing medium to put between the slabs, and what would you suggest I plant? The patio does get sun for some of the day in summer.
Terry, Suffolk

I am presuming no prancing labradors/no children's bikes and scooters, then. Diana Ross (the garden writer) had for a time a fabulous-looking but totally impractical terrace outside her Clapham house where lofty *Verbena bonariensis* had seeded between every crack. And I have seen a very yummy grand-but-crumbly terrace awash with a froth of that dear old standby lady's mantle (*Alchemilla mollis*), too.

The best medium? Loam-based John Innes No 2 (No 3 would be OK, but a bit rock-like when dry – not so hospitable to seeding plants).

The best plants? Well that depends somewhat on the amount of sun (of which there will obviously be much less near the house). I would suggest trying Spanish daisy (*Erigeron karvinskianus* – see also June, page 64) in the sunniest parts and an acaena (New Zealand burr) of some sort (*A. microphylla* 'Copper Carpet' looks great with the daisy) that will creep happily into the shade. You don't sound like the sort of gardener who throws up their hands (believe me, some do) at the idea of cultivating little yellow and orange Welsh poppies (*Meconopsis cambrica*), which will seed around even in deep shade, can be cut back at any time in the summer and re-flower endlessly. Planting the acaena is easy if you slot in small plants at the 'crossroads' between four slabs, from whence it will creep in all directions. ❦

DISGUISING A SEPTIC TANK

I have recently downshifted to a considerably smaller garden where the septic tank has been put in a fairly conspicuous position – in a north-facing site, backed by a fence. My predecessor had surrounded it with a wooden curb and covered it with gravel. Please can you help me to find some way of obscuring it?
Carolyn, Somerset

I can't help feeling that the previous owners of your property may have done what I am about to suggest that you do: use a difficult area as a 'stage' for something eye-catching.

In a sunny, open site it would be quite easy to follow a fairly traditional route: think bird bath, lavender or herbs around the edge of the area to eventually hide the timber framework. Not scintillatingly original, but efficient and easy on the eye.

However, given the shade and the fence (which you could try to hide with evergreens), I would suggest that you do what I have done in a part of my garden (backed by a hedge and under a yew) where it is impossible to grow anything in the ground. I have collected several rather handsome pots and urns over the years and these I have grouped together and planted up with an assortment of contrasting leafy and quite shade-tolerant plants – some evergreen, permanent and almost immovable, others that come and go with the seasons.

199

Clipped box balls of different sizes form the backbone, with hostas, *Melianthus major*, cannas, castor oil plants (*Ricinus communis*), colourful cordylines, ferns, kirengeshoma and even, one year, a huge banana plant, are also included in the mix. It isn't really as high maintenance as it sounds, and in fact I rather enjoy thinking up new ways of dressing the area up each year. There are pictures of this on my blog (helenyemm.com) which might be helpful. ❦

SAME 'PAPER WHITES' NEXT YEAR?

Now that my fabulous indoor display of 'Paper White' narcissi has finished flowering, can I plant the bulbs outside to die back? Will they flower again next year outside or can I dry them and bring them back for another indoor display next winter?
Barbara, by email

There is a problem with either of these options where indoor-flowering spring bulbs are concerned. The 'Paper Whites' such as those you enjoyed are extremely pernickety. To perform the way they do, when they do, they are carefully nurtured and specially 'forced' by the growers. If you simply plant the bulbs in the ground now, letting them die back naturally as you would other bulbs, they simply refuse to flower again. And even if you treat them with what might seem to be a bit more TLC, feeding them while letting their leaves die back indoors, then drying out the bulbs before replanting them late next autumn, they will do no better I am afraid. Hyacinths are slightly more accommodating, incidentally. They will eventually settle down and may flower annually outdoors, but the flowers will become skinnier by the year and end up resembling rather unremarkable bluebells (or pink or whitebells) more than their blowsy former selves.

I occasionally advocate what is considered by some to

be out and out profligacy on various gardening matters, but I recommend strongly that in order to save yourself unnecessary effort and heartache you should treat your 'Paper Whites' as annuals, chuck them out (not on the compost bin, where they might sprout annoyingly just to spite you) and simply buy new ones for next winter's scent-fest. After all – and I have said this before, too – we need to remind ourselves that half a dozen or so narcissi bulbs cost less than a bunch of (equally disposable) cut flowers. 🌿

BYE BYE DAPHNE

This month should be declared National Daphne Month, judging by the contents of my stuffed inbox. Doreen from Hertfordshire has a magnificent somewhat prostrate *Daphne tangutica* that is doing so well it is now slumping all over her lawn. Given that she has an unheated greenhouse she can use, how and when should she try to take cuttings from it, so that it can eventually be replaced? Daphnes are extremely slow growing and are generally regarded as hard to propagate, but Doreen should certainly give it a go, preparing for the event right now by cutting a few branches of the old plant back by a few inches to encourage it to make some good new shoots from which to take several cuttings later on. The time to do the deed is late summer, and Doreen should take several short heel cuttings, a few inches long, removing all but the top leaves before dipping them in hormone rooting powder, then poking them into free-draining cuttings compost. Moisture is crucial for the first few months – the unheated greenhouse may be a bit too hot and dry in late summer, so a sheltered spot out of the sun in the garden might be better. Also – nothing ventured, nothing gained – since her existing plant is somewhat prostrate, she could try a technique called 'layering', inducing a shoot or shoots that are touching the ground to produce roots by carefully nicking a few stems close to a leaf and pegging them down to the ground.

'Garden envy' can eat away at us. Dot's neighbour has a vigorous, young, new *Daphne odora*, while her own 13-year-old plant has recently become, for want of a better description, threadbare, with small yellowing lower leaves and not much in the way of new growth or flowers. Both are growing in south-facing gardens; why is her plant so shabby? New, tunnel-grown, much-nurtured plants always look lush. Dot's plant simply looks old and starved to me and may, after 13 years, have simply run out of steam. Maybe Dot should be taking cuttings (from her neighbour's plant?) too.

Daphne's *Daphne odora*, which has this winter suddenly for the first time got brown tips to its leaves, probably suffered from frost damage after she knocked the snow off its branches. Unless branches of tender-ish evergreens become so laden with snow that they are in danger of splitting under its weight, it is best to leave them covered with the stuff rather than expose them to icy winds (see also January, page 183).

Yet another Daphne, from Taunton, wants to know if there is a summer-flowering/fragrant variety. *Daphne × transatlantica* 'Eternal Fragrance' is the one – flowering from spring for most of the summer.

SNOWDROPS AND NETTLES

A large area of woodland next to our garden is a glorious show of snowdrops now but in a few weeks the area will be covered with dense nettles. We normally garden organically but this wood is defeating me. If we sprayed would the snowdrops be killed?
Fidelity, Berwick, Northumberland

Digging out the shallow roots of nettles, although not difficult, is not an option here because you would disturb the snowdrop population, of course. However, it should not be too difficult to get rid of the nettles using a glyphosate-based weedkiller such as Roundup, which does not linger in the soil. Some organic gardeners – but not the 'purists', of course – find its use acceptable in cases of extreme necessity, which this seems to be.

Timing is crucial, since glyphosate acts through contact

with leaves: you will have to wait for the snowdrop foliage to die back completely – by which time the weed invasion will be well under way. The most effective way to treat nettles is to strim them in early summer and wait until their re-growth is about 8in (20cm) high, before thoroughly spraying (or watering) the foliage with the glyphosate solution on a dry and sunny day. Nettles spread by seed as well as via invasive shallow roots, so one treatment won't get you out of the wood, as the expression goes. 🌿

ALL WHITE EVENTUALLY

I have always loved the spinney of white-stemmed birches at Anglesey Abbey in Cambridgeshire, and so when the opportunity arose recently (after the felling of a weeping willow), I planted a couple of Betula utilis *var.* jacquemontii *in the corner of our suburban garden, each of them 6–7ft (1.8–2.1m) high. Disappointingly, they do not seem to have any inclination to develop that lovely white bark. How long will I have to wait?*
J F, New Barnet, Greater London

It is hard to be precise about this – but rest assured that these lovely trees do take a little time to develop their startlingly white bark. It sounds as though they were sold as very young trees. At 6ft (1.8m) tall, they may be only three or four years old at most, and perhaps you will have to be patient for another three or four years before they gradually lose their bronzy-brown bark, which will peel off to reveal their true, white beauty. To persuade them to grow as fast as possible, make sure they are not competing with grass or other plants around their feet, and give them a spring feed each year with a general fertiliser such as blood, fish and bone. It is amazing how much difference a little TLC makes to the growth rate of young trees. 🌿

AND FINALLY...

A touch of grumpiness caused by the following all too familiar lack of information.

I am concerned that my hydrangea might be a casualty of last winter. It is showing no sign of budding. Could you please advise whether my fears are right or are my expectations too early?
Ian, by email

Well honestly! Without knowing where you live (north or south) or where the hydrangea is situated in your garden (exposed or not...), or roughly what kind of hydrangea it is, this is too tricky a question to answer properly. Certainly in the south-east my mop-heads are already coming into leaf and also showing signs of new growth coming from the base. But other types (*H. paniculata* 'Brussels Lace' and *H. arborescens* 'Annabelle', for example), that flower on all-new wood and were therefore recently pruned quite hard, are still barely getting going.

I think you would do well, however, to wait a while. There is a good chance that even if your *Hydrangea whateveritis* was severely damaged by frost, new growth will come from around the base – which may or may not flower this year depending on whatever it is. Harrumph. 🌿

THINGS TO CONSIDER IN FEBRUARY

Late winter clipping and snipping
🌿 Aim to finish pruning bush roses (Hybrid Teas, Floribundas, Modern Shrubs) by the beginning of next month.

🌿 Late-flowering clematis (e.g. Viticella Group and 'Bill MacKenzie') can be cut right back now to around 18in (45cm) from the ground.

204

❋ Take the shears to established lavender, cutting back a substantial part of the grey foliage making them into neat grey hedgehogs, but don't cut them back into old wood. Similarly treat perovskia.

❋ Prune out obviously dead or damaged wood from dormant shrubs and small trees that are prone to die-back, e.g. ornamental acers.

❋ Snip away the papery remains of last year's flower heads from climbing hydrangeas before they annoy you by blowing all over the garden.

❋ Spring clean sword-leaved evergreen perennials such as golden oats (*Stipa gigantea*) and *Libertia grandiflora* by cutting out old flower stems and browning foliage and raking out trapped autumn leaves.

Start feeding
❋ Feed roses with a proprietary rose food then apply a mulch, making sure that neither comes into direct contact with the base branches.

❋ Also start to feed and mulch other flowering shrubs: rose food works well for these too.

Other bits and pieces
❋ Pinch out sweet pea seedlings that were sown in autumn under glass.

❋ Cut back last year's overwintered pelargoniums and re-pot them using soil-based compost. Take cuttings from the best trimmings.

Directory of Suppliers

Many of the products mentioned in the text are available from your local garden centre. If you can't find a stockist for a specific product, consult the list below.

Algae & Mould Stain Cleaner see *Biotal*

Anti-Acid Lime Mix for wormeries see *Wiggly Wigglers*

Arboricultural Association trees.org.uk

Baby Bio House Plant Insecticide see *Bayer*

Barley straw bales see *Wiggly Wigglers*

Bayer products go to bayergarden.co.uk and click on store locator

Biotal products from organiccatalogue.com

Bordeaux Mixture see *Vitax*

Bosch cordless leaf blower for more information go to bosch-garden.com/

Bosmere Tip Bag various online stockists, including tesco.com and amazon.co.uk

BugClear insecticides see *Scotts*

Chafer Grub Killer see *Nemasys*

Dansand for stockists contact dansand.co.uk

David Austin roses davidaustinroses.com 01902 376300

Doff Knockdown Maxi Strength Weedkiller doff.co.uk/stockists 0115 983 4300

Encarsia formosa available from various suppliers, including harrodhorticultural.com 0845 402 5300 and greengardener.co.uk 01493 750061

Extract of Barley Straw from ecopond.co.uk 01225 767919

Flexi-Tie from flexi-tie.co.uk 01629 636945

FungusClear Ultra see *Scotts*

Grazers deer repellent from grazers.co.uk

Growmore see *Vitax*

Jakoti shears from handshears.co.uk 01749 938008

Japanese knotweed go to environment-agency.gov.uk and type Japanese knotweed in the search box

Lawn sand from gardenscapedirect.co.uk 0800 854663 or 01797 253666

Maxicrop seaweed fertilisers go to maxicrop.co.uk and click on 'Where to get Maxicrop' 08700 115117

Miracle-Gro see *Scotts*

Multirose Bug Killer see *Bayer*

Nemasys range available from various suppliers, including harrodhorticultural.com and greengardener.co.uk

No Ants see *Nemasys*

Provado Ultimate Bug Killer Ready to Use and *Provado Ultimate Bug Killer 2* see *Bayer*

Provado Vine Weevil Killer 2 see *Bayer*

RHS Supreme Green Lawn Seed with Rootgrow various online stockists, including tesco.com and amazon.co.uk

Rootgrow online from rootgrow.co.uk or click on 'store finder' 01795 411527

Roundup Ultra 3000 go to roundup-garden.com and click on 'Where to buy?'

Roundup Weedkiller Gel as above

Scotts products from lovethegarden.com 0845 1901881

Sequestrene see *Scotts*

SlugClear see *Scotts*

Slug Gone see *Vitax*

Sulphate of iron and *Sulphate of potash* see *Vitax*

Super Strength Glyphosate see *Bayer*

Systhane Fungus Fighter see *Bayer*

Tough Rootkill see *Bayer*

Vine Weevil Killer see *Nemasys*

Vitax products go to vitax.co.uk/home-garden/where-to-buy/

Wiggly Wigglers wormery supplies from wigglywigglers.co.uk 01981 500391

Information correct at time of going to press.

Index

Note: Common names are preferred, except in those cases where the scientific name alone appears in the text.

Acknowledgements

I have many individuals and organisations to thank for this, the second volume of 'Thorny Problems'.

To start with, organisations: My thanks are due to the decision-makers at *The Daily Telegraph* who continued to give space to a traditional weekly gardening letters page in the face of the great internet earthquake that continues to cause tremors of insecurity throughout the world of the printed word. I am also grateful to the powers that be at Simon & Schuster who, together with Telegraph Books, put their shoulders behind this little project and gently shoved. I am grateful, too, to the RHS for their continued goodwill and help (and, incidentally, for their brilliant website) and to manufacturers and suppliers of all sorts of gardening hardware for their support.

And individuals? My thanks of course go to Joanna Fortnam, gardening editor of the Saturday *Telegraph*, and to her equally amiable assistant Ed Cumming, for morale-boosting support when at times forests of readers' dying bay trees, flocks of scale insects and armies of honey fungus toadstools threatened to overwhelm my weekly garden-writing mojo.

And of course, I am totally indebted, again, to the book-creators at Simon & Schuster: To brilliantly organised editor Sharon Amos, who has again helped me to re-work readers' problems and my solutions into something really pleasing and, I hope, horticulturally helpful; to illustrator Francine Lawrence, whose little drawings are sprinkled like sequins throughout the text, and the design team who, as before, have stitched the whole thing together so beautifully. And I mustn't miss out Lorraine Jerram, project editor at Simon & Schuster, who has clearly done really, really well, and with great enthusiasm, whatever it is project editors do!

Lastly, my heartfelt thanks go to all those fraught but endlessly friendly *Telegraph* gardeners, without whom... I might well have starved.

ALSO BY HELEN YEMM AND PUBLISHED
BY SIMON & SCHUSTER ILLUSTRATED

'I have always loved reading Helen's column in The Telegraph – to have a whole book of garden questions with her sensible and humorous answers is an absolute joy. Thank you.'

'Helen, as always, is very readable... I have been gardening for over 30 years and she can still teach me a thing or two!'

'If you like gardening it's interesting to read about problems! And solve some of your own. Always more to learn in gardening – and here is heaps of experience shared with us, and balanced, sensible advice. I would gladly buy a complete collection of the Telegraph column, so more please!'

'This is a delightful book. It brings together everything you might need to know to achieve successful and enjoyable gardening and in the most lively and engaging manner possible. It should appeal to all gardeners, pyjama-clad or otherwise.'

'Helen Yemm is the only REALLY down-to-earth gardener who appreciates a beginner (and idiot) and explains everything so clearly.'

'I love this book, it is so informative and helpful. Many topics made me laugh out loud and I recommend this book to all gardeners.'

A selection of Amazon customer reviews